ROOTED

MURRAY ANDREW PURA

ROOTED

REFLECTIONS *on the* GARDENS *in* SCRIPTURE

ZONDERVAN®

ZONDERVAN.com/
AUTHORTRACKER
follow your favorite authors

ZONDERVAN

Rooted
Copyright © 2010 by Murray Andrew Pura

This title is also available as a Zondervan ebook. Visit www.zondervan.com/ebooks.

This title is also available in a Zondervan audio edition. Visit www.zondervan.fm.

Requests for information should be addressed to:

Zondervan, *Grand Rapids, Michigan* 49530

Library of Congress Cataloging-in-Publication Data

Pura, Murray, 1954–
     Rooted: reflections on the gardens in Scripture / Murray Andrew Pura.
          p.   cm.
     Includes bibliographical references.
     ISBN 978-0-310-31837-8
     1. Gardens in the Bible I. Title.
     BS665.P87   2009
     220.8'635 – dc22   2009028909

Cover design: Studio Gearbox
Cover photo: Getty Images® / Roine Magnusson
Interior design: Michelle Espinoza

Printed in the United States of America

---

10 11 12 13 14 15 • 23 22 21 20 19 18 17 16 15 14 13 12 11 10 9 8 7 6 5 4 3 2 1

*for J. I. Packer in his eighth decade,
still digging deeply into God's Word
and unearthing for us wisdom
planted before the beginning of time*

*and for my wife's father and mother,
Richard and Goldie Levy,
gardeners in earth's soil and God's words*

CONTENTS

FOREWORD

by Eugene Peterson

As you open this book and begin to read what is written here, you are about to find yourself in a garden of nouns and verbs, commas and semicolons, sentences and paragraphs, and enough strategically placed periods to provide the necessary rest stops for taking in the profusion of shapes and colors and fragrances—and perhaps to occasionally pull up a fingerling carrot or pick a raspberry and savor its taste.

Murray Pura is a gardener. He and his wife, Linda, have planted gardens wherever they have lived in Canada and the United States. But as is true of many, maybe most, gardeners, they have not only planted and worked their gardens; they have immersed themselves in both seasonal rhythms and unseasonable weather, in the sensual and earthy reciprocities of hard work and delicious rest. They have *enjoyed* these gardens.

. But here is the best part: all these gardens have their roots in five gardens planted and tended by God. *All* of the gardens we plant have their ancestry in God's gardens.

Murray Pura is also a pastor. He has spent a vocational lifetime making himself thoroughly at home in God's five gardens all the while he has planted and harvested his own garden and cultivated the congregational gardens in which God has commanded him to "work the ground and keep it in order" (Genesis 2:15).

God's five gardens—Eden, En Gedi, Gethsemane, Garden Tomb, Second Eden—offer themselves not only as a comprehensive metaphor for understanding the delightful intricacies in which God works with us and we share in his work but as a much-needed way to read Scripture (and our own lives) slowly, reflectively, believingly (that is, as participants), and prayerfully. Murray takes the offer, and in a remarkable fusion of pastor and writer, poet and exegete, gardener and friend, he invites us to join him as a leisurely companion in entering into God's ways with us in creation and salvation, in our daily work and our Sabbath worship.

No one needs this kind of assistance as much as we do today. This world of incessant distraction, noise, and frenzied hurry puts us under constant threat of being depersonalized into functions or problems or consumers. Our God-created, image-of-God capacity for prayer and delight, beauty and belief, forgiveness and holiness, gradually but surely leaks out of us. Our souls are desiccated. The results are ominous—anger and violence, anxiety and depression, narcissism and addictions.

One of the more serious fallouts that come from growing up and living in these conditions is that we read the Bible as fast as we can for what we can get out of it on our own terms. But we cannot read Scripture in a hurry any more than we can cultivate a garden in a hurry. When we rip the Scriptures out of their context—this long, patient, creative, redemptive, and compassionate cultivation in the gardens of God—we desecrate the Scriptures and do severe damage to our own souls.

This is serious. We need serious help. *Rooted* is serious — but in no way somber. The joy of the gospel permeates it.

> Eugene Peterson, professor emeritus
> of spiritual theology, Regent College,
> Vancouver, BC, Canada,
> and translator of *The Message*

I think that if ever a mortal heard the voice of God, it would be in a garden at the cool of the day.

F. Frankfort Moore, *A Garden of Peace*

THE GARDEN PATH

I was twenty-five years old before I found out I had a cousin who was a monk living in a monastery in the south end of the city. No one in the family had ever mentioned him. It was a mutual friend who figured it out. He set up a meeting, and I showed up at the big iron gates and high walls of the monastery at the appointed time. I pulled a rope, a bell clanged, and a figure cloaked in white and black came, greeted me, and brought me inside to the Father Abbot.

I confess I was a bit apprehensive about meeting my cousin. After all, what did we have in common? He was Catholic, I was Protestant; he had taken a vow of chastity, I hoped to meet a young woman and get married; he spent his days isolated from the world in the monastery, I spent my days right in the middle of the world. For that matter, what did I have in common with any of the men who moved silently in and out of the abbot's office in black hoods and white robes?

But there was nothing to worry about. The abbot plied me with homemade cookies and glasses of fresh milk from the monastery's prize dairy herd—"Do you want another cookie? How about some more milk? What do you think of it? How does it taste? Is it cold enough for you?" When my cousin finally arrived, he was full of smiles and warmth and looked like Friar Tuck. Even though among themselves the Trappists maintained a vow of silence a large part of the time, with visitors they were allowed to speak freely. And laugh freely—which my cousin, Brother Martin, found very easy to do.

He took me on a tour of the monastery—down long stone corridors to the chapel, to the library, to the kitchen. We talked about family, about faith, about God. I told him about my work with a street church in the downtown area, and he exclaimed, "This is great. You're out there ministering to people, and I'm in here praying for you!" The abbot popped up and gave me an old book on prayer by Francis de Sales. I talked to brothers who were milking the prize cows and who cracked jokes with me. The afternoon sped past, and I was just heading out the gates when my cousin came running down the path calling my name: "Wait! Can you stay for supper? The brothers would love to have you as our guest!"

So I stayed and ate fresh bread, drank more milk, helped myself to that great Trappist invention, Oka cheese, had some pop, watched the young brothers eat and grin and pass bowls of salad back and forth along the long wooden table, and, after another hour or two, said my good-byes and went home quietly in joy, one last time retracing my steps down the garden path to the front gates.

My cousin had walked me along that garden path alongside which there were daisies and dill and long full rows of cabbage and lettuce and carrots and beets. Trappists are vegetarians, so the garden is an important resource. It is not only one of the great essentials of their physical life; it is also critical for their spiritual sustenance. In the gardens they hoe and pray; in the gardens they walk and read Scripture; in the gardens they sit and meditate on God and worship.

Speckled by rain that summer Saturday, dark and green and unfolding, I was reminded as I walked the path that Christians had kept monasteries for almost two thousand years, and on and around the grounds of those monasteries they had grazed cattle, harvested grain, and planted gardens of flowers, vegetables, and herbs. The wonder was that this day, among a group of modern-day monks, I had taken some of that growth into me and, in their company, nourished both my body and my spirit.

The Bible has its own garden path. It runs from Genesis to Revelation. In fact, some of the most important events in the Christian faith take place in biblical gardens, events around which Christianity has established its doctrines as firmly as great rocks in the sand. Many of us have known these crucial teachings of the Christian faith since we were children—the fall into sin in the Garden of Eden, Christ's night of sorrow in the Garden of Gethsemane, his resurrection from the dead at the Garden Tomb—yes, we know these teachings by heart.

Or maybe not by heart. How do the great teachings of Scripture get from our heads to our hearts and souls and make a difference in our ordinary lives? It is the gardens we find in the Bible that actually help these teachings hit home by bringing them down to earth. We can sift them through our fingers and bring them to our nostrils like good soil and smell in them the strength and health and vigor that bring the miraculous into our world.

Think about it. "God Almighty first planted a garden,"

writes Francis Bacon, who was born in 1561, "and, indeed, it is the purest of human pleasures; it is the greatest refreshment to the spirits of man."[*]

God first planted a garden. He is given many names in the Bible — grand names, majestic names — but from the beginning to the end there is one name more illuminating than the rest by which we can know him: God is a gardener. In Genesis 2:8, we are told, "God had planted a garden in the east." Immediately we get an image of the Deity stooping down from the high heavens to dig out a hole in the ground for a maple sapling or an evergreen, eventually dropping to his knees to grub about in the soil. He is doing the things we do in gardens — or we've seen others do: patting earth firmly around the base of a newly planted chokecherry bush, spreading the roots of a petunia, placing carrot seeds, watering. There is mud under his fingernails, mud under his skin, mud streaked under the sockets of his eyes. "The LORD God made all kinds of trees grow out of the ground — trees that were pleasing to the eye and good for food" (verse 9). I suppose you could say God did not get dirty at all; he simply spoke the garden into existence, as Genesis 1 tells us: "God said, 'Let the land produce vegetation: seed-bearing plants and trees on the land that bear fruit with seed in it, according to their various kinds.' And it was so" (Genesis 1:11).

I hesitate, however, to interpret Genesis 1 as meaning that God is anything less than up close and personal with his creation. Yes, God does speak things into existence and declares

---

[*] Samuel Harvey Reynolds, ed., *The Essays or Counsels, Civil and Moral of Francis Bacon* (Oxford: Clarendon, 1890), 321.

matters to be so, but then he goes about getting intimately involved in what he has just voiced. In Genesis 2, we are treated to a frame-by-frame playback after the big picture in Genesis 1. We get a sense of God in Genesis 2 not as distant and transcendent but as hands-on with what he has made. God is bent over in the dust, on all fours, shaping a human out of the ground, placing divine lips over nostrils of dirt and breathing in the breath of life so that his sculpture of clay and mud becomes a living creature (2:7). In Genesis 1, he says, "Let us make human beings in our image, in our likeness" (1:26 TNIV); in Genesis 2, he rolls up his sleeves and does it. Do we find that Genesis 2 tells us God merely speaks the garden into existence? No, we are told he plants it. How does the first human get into this garden? By a spoken command? No, God puts him there: "The LORD God took the man and put him in the Garden of Eden to work it and take care of it" (2:15). Our image of a gardening God with dirt up to his elbows and involved in his creation, body and soul, is not so whimsical after all but is the real thing.

And why not? What is the Son of God coming to earth, except deity taking on nostrils of dirt or legs and arms of dust? What is our salvation, but Christ planted dead in the ground like a seed and then bursting into life, cracking the crust of earth and night and bringing daybreak to the world? Isn't it striking that Mary Magdalene, setting her eyes on Jesus for the first time after the resurrection, thinks he's a gardener (John 20:15)? It's equally striking that the Bible goes full circle and ends where it begins—with a garden that God makes and in which humans live:

Look! God's dwelling place is now among the people, and he will dwell with them. They will be his people, and God himself will be with them and be their God....

Then the angel showed me the river of the water of life, as clear as crystal, flowing from the throne of God and of the Lamb down the middle of the great street of the city. On each side of the river stood the tree of life, bearing twelve crops of fruit, yielding its fruit every month. And the leaves of the tree are for the healing of the nations.

Revelation 21:3; 22:1–2 TNIV

In the beginning, the Garden of Eden holds within its borders everything about the destiny and possibilities of human existence. The end of the Bible is this promise fulfilled in a second Eden. The first Eden is like a seed, carrying all that is necessary for humans to coexist in harmony with the earth and all that is upon it, including the Divine Being who fashioned the whole of it. The second Eden of heaven is the tree fully grown, without any danger of rot or disease or fire or flood bringing it down. But Eden in all its fullness is impossible without Eden in its infancy and fragility.

We know the story. The first Eden fell. But the spiritual Eden is with us still; it is the story of the entire human race and all of creation — all plants and animals and birds, all the sea and all the sky and all the glittering night. Because of the first Eden, the first garden, the Gardener will come to earth, clearly visible to all but unknown to most, and he will cause Eden to become what it was always meant to become—heaven on earth. How will he do this? The way all gardeners have it in them to restore a garden that has been overrun and reclaimed by the wild. He will weed. He will prune. He will replenish the soil. He will hoe and till. He will nurture it back to life so that the garden will unfold like a rose. Ultimately, he will water the soil with his blood.

All this we would never experience except for the first Eden and the tragedy that drove humans from it. We would never know the lengths to which God would go to give us another life. We would never know how much he loved that race whose nostrils he had kissed and into whom he had breathed the air of his own immortality and inextinguishable light. "How great a Fall," wrote Augustine, "that merited so great a Redeemer."

The Bible is studded with references to sowing seed and growing crops and planting vineyards. But there are five passages that stand out—one in Genesis, one in the Song of Songs, two in the Gospels, and a final one in the Revelation to John. They are the five gardens of God, and the signs above their gates read: Eden, En Gedi, Gethsemane, the Garden Tomb, and the garden of heaven—Second Eden. To walk through these gardens is to walk the garden path. And just like the monastic gardens, they are much more than places where flowers and herbs grow. They are icons of the Father, Son, and Holy Spirit; they are images of the transcendent, windows to heaven, metaphors of the spiritual life. Their roots must penetrate us and reach down into our very souls, and the gardens themselves must be planted in us. Each one is a spiritual environment of such vitality and color and wisdom that we need to enter them in prayer and meditation to seek God, to ask questions of the Gardener, to listen, to worship, to struggle, to be at peace. The biblical gardens are a place of encounter with the Holy Spirit, "the Greening Power of God," as Hildegard of Bingen called him.

But the gardens are more than images and metaphors and symbols of the Christian faith. God's gardens are stories, and these stories are all double-edged and triple-edged. They have meanings behind the obvious meanings. Trees may take on deeper significance. Fruit may stand for more than oranges or pears or grapes. Blood may be more than blood and do things ordinary blood cannot do. Animals may not be animals. Henna blossoms may not be henna blossoms. Death may not be death. Even the Maker of heaven and earth is known by different identities—a creator in one garden, a lover in another, a victim in yet another.

The biblical gardens offer us stories that can take us "further up and further in"—the words Aslan spoke to encourage the boys and girls to plunge deeper into the mysteries and wonders of Narnia. As we stand among the gardens' trees and plants and bright waters and shadows, we begin to feel there was some truth to all of the fairy tales we were told when we were children, all the stories about princes and princesses, cunning sorcerers and powerful spells, all the tales of hidden jewels and towering castles and great creatures with flapping wings, all the fantasy epics that teem with flashing swords and enchanted gardens and talking beasts and thorns and thistles and banishment. We realize they were more than fantastical flights of the imagination; they were flights to the core of our existence. There is something in us that wishes to tell these stories, and there is something in us that wishes to hear them. When these stories are told, we relish the battle between good and evil, light and darkness, courage and cowardice, death and immortality.

Outwardly we may pretend to laugh off all the images of dark and light: "It's just a story." But inwardly we turn the themes of these childhood tales over and over in our minds and hearts. Before the dark of sleep. Gazing at a sunset that is a conflagration of cloud and flame. Silent in front of a blazing fire where the coals glitter like the stones of a magic palace. Alone at the stroke of midnight under the white stars of heaven. On a beach where the sea storm crashes into rock and sand, and wind stings at your face and hands.

No, the best fairy tales are not just stories. They are speaking about things that exist, but they are speaking cryptically. They are in costume. We are not always certain what may be hidden behind the mask and colorful garments. Something is going on, but we can't quite get the whole of it. We reach out and grab on to bits and pieces. One part of the tale is about integrity, another about deceit. That character embodies the sacred, this other character the unholy. The quest for the grail is a quest for the divine. The destruction of the Ring is the destruction of selfishness and lust and obsession, the vicious things we cling to and that cling to us. We come to believe that the greatest of these stories mean much more than they appear to mean on the surface, and that they represent deeper truths that are a part of our existence—truths seen and unseen.

In the biblical gardens, drops of sweat can turn into drops of blood, a dead man can come back to life. We do not just come to a rosebush or a peach tree when we come to God's gardens, but to a whole world—physical, metaphysical, natural, supernatural, skin and bone and heart and spirit. Everything that matters is in these gardens; everything we feel—ecstasy, anguish—has a niche, everything that puzzles, all that inspires. The gardens are all of life and all of God.

There is one great difference between the fairy tales and the stories from the Bible, however. The fairy tales show us things that are true, but the tales themselves are not real. Real persons do not get hurt. The evil in the fairy tales vanishes into air, into thin air. In the Bible, the stories are for real, and real people do get hurt—women, children, men, even God. And the gardens in which so many stories take place are not illusions or special effects—they have real soil, real plants, real stones. The gardens are real, and the people, the angels, the devils, and the divine in them are real also.

As we look at these gardens together, we will take each one as a whole. There may be a place for trying to figure out the symbolism of each plant or gardening tool used in the Bible, just as there may be a place for trying to nail down the hidden significance of every item and aspect of the tabernacle the children of Israel used in the desert. "Every natural fact," says Emerson, "is a symbol of some spiritual fact." We could say that when Isaiah talks about refashioning swords into plows, the plow is a symbol of opening soil rather than opening veins and ought to be seen as God's call to peace. We could say that shovels in biblical stories stand for plantings, for spiritual beginnings, for cultivation, restoration, and rejuvenation.

A seed is spiritual possibility. It is also the tiniest amount of faith, and a mustard plant symbolizes the miraculous growth of that small and slender hope. A Mexican friar, Emmanuel de Villegas, described how each part of the passion flower symbolized something about the passion of Christ — the pointed leaves are the spear thrust into his side, the red stigma the nails stained with his blood, and so on. If we were to take this approach to the five gardens of God, we would soon be overwhelmed by a deluge of fragmentary information — some of it marginal, some of it absurd, some of it no doubt useful, but a good bit of it little more than smoke and mirrors. No, it is better that we come to the gardens seeking an atmosphere in which to think and pray and wonder rather than one in which to play a biblical Trivial Pursuit — to focus on God in his wholeness rather than on the little bits and pieces, however bright and shining, that fall from his hands as he passes.

All we need to do is walk the garden path. Spend time in Eden, spend time in Gethsemane, stand still before an empty grave in a spring garden alive with honeybees and hummingbirds, yes, and alive with something much more. A day, an hour spent in these gardens can change a life and help us see what we may never have seen, or see it again, or see it in a way we never saw it before. And, if the light is right, see God in a way we never saw him before. Perhaps the playwright George Bernard Shaw said it best, and though I think he said it with a smile, I think he also said it because he had been there and knew it was true: "The best place to seek God is in a garden. You can dig for him there."*

---

* George Bernard Shaw, *The Black Girl in Search of God* (New York: Samuel French, 1977), 51.

PART ONE

EDEN

The GARDEN *of* BIRTH

The LORD God had planted a garden
in the east, in Eden.
Genesis 2:8

ONE

Rain slashed and wind cut and ocean waves thumped against the rocks and sand and stones. The night was cold and without stars, without moon, without light of any kind. Two men and a woman walked back and forth across a stretch of grass that sloped to the sea, hunched against the sting of the storm. A flashlight beam jumped up and down and illuminated shining grass and swinging trees. The wind seemed to grab the beam and hurl it from one side of the strip of land to the other. Out over the dark water were the chop of waves against boats and the snap of rigging against aluminum spars and the creak of cables pulling hard at their moorings. And farther out still the grunt and groan of a foghorn.

"You say it's two acres?" asked one of the men to the other. Water streamed down his glasses.

The man with the flashlight nodded. "From the highway right down to the cove."

"What about water?" asked the woman.

"You'll have to sink a well. But all the wells along this shore have sweet water. That's not a problem."

"The cove seems pretty sheltered even with this storm going on," said the man with the glasses as he looked out toward the ocean.

"Yeah, it would take a hurricane to really give you trouble tucked away in here."

"We'll take it then."

"You'll take it?"

The woman smiled and nodded, her hood and face wet with rain. "You bet we'll take it."

The man with the flashlight shook his head. "You walk around the property on the dirtiest night of the year, you can't see your hand in front of your face — why, it's like buying the place sight unseen."

They laughed — and began to walk up the grassy slope toward their cars as the wind and rain continued to pound their heads and backs.

"You have a bunch of people waiting to see this property in the morning, am I right?" asked the man with the glasses.

"I sure do."

"We had to beat them to the punch."

"Well, you did that. Nobody else wanted to come out until after the storm had blown through. I'll have to call them all and tell them they can save themselves a trip."

"I guess you will."

The two men stopped by the cars and shook hands in the dark.

Once the storm had passed, the sun shone again and the sea glittered white and blue at the foot of the property like a net of gems. Over a period of weeks and months, a well was drilled, a dock built and moored securely in the cove, a house erected and filled with furniture. But what the man and his wife had looked forward to most came in May—the opportunity to split open the grass and plant a garden.

Day after day, their spades and picks cut apart the earth. Their mattocks and machinery turned the soil. They sweated and toiled and grunted and grinned. Halfway down the long slope of grass they planted a large vegetable plot. A strawberry patch was put there too. Near the plot they placed fruit trees. A grapevine. Raspberry canes. Dirt jammed under their fingernails and streaked black across their foreheads. Closer to the house they marked out flower gardens with orange, pink, and purple petals. Roses. Herbs. They changed the land. They altered the colors of the earth. And they thought it was good, very good. So did many others.

When you change your world, some things are diminished, some things are added. There was less grass on their property, though still plenty to go around, less white and red clover, less wide-open spaces. But the bees were in heaven, a heaven that had not existed for them before. Hummingbirds showed up, playing the air like a Stradivarius. Butterflies with pale blue wings arrived and rested on the highest daisies. Deer ate the lettuce, crows ate the corn. Robins came for worms. Blackbirds for berries. Chipmunks raided the feeding stations set up for sparrows and cardinals and nuthatches. Flies arrived also. But close on their wings came dragonflies of metallic green and emerald. Snakes without venom slid between flower stalks. Visitors made tea from fresh spearmint leaves. The gardens gave both humans and the creatures about them much pleasure. The gardens fed their bodies. Even with the hard work of weeding, the gardens offered a new happiness.

This was the garden of my wife's parents, Richard and Goldie, a garden built by the sea. Before their arrival, the waters of the Atlantic, for the most part, splashed against an untouched shoreline of earth and stone. For hundreds of years, thousands of years, the grass had not been turned. The soil had rested from generation to generation. The property looked perfect just the way it was—emerald field sloping down to rock and sand beach, trees tall, jade leaves gleaming, salt waters flashing as if the stars had fallen. But Richard and Goldie felt something was missing. Gardens. So they began to create them.

Not all gardens may be fenced. But all gardens have definite boundaries. There are edges to them, just as there are edges between sea and sky and land and ocean. They are separate from the world around them, even though they haven't gone anywhere. A garden stands out. As lovely as the land around us might be, we notice gardens immediately—beauty within beauty.

It is in us to do what Richard and Goldie did. To plant. Create. Not only gardens of the ground but gardens of the mind and of the spirit, gardens of music and gardens of words and gardens of worship. In all of these gardens, I think, we are trying to find Eden again. Eden is an old memory we cannot recall except by glimpses of what our hands and imaginations do pretty much out of thin air, surprising us. "I never knew you had it in you," someone tells us while admiring our handiwork. Neither did we. The paint of Eden is in the violets and orchids we plant and admire. The music of Eden is in the melodies of the guitarist and the pianist and the cellist. The drama of Eden is in some of our finest plays and films. The sweetness we create. The symmetry. The prayers. The paradise. Something deep inside each one of us wants the first garden again. Something in us wants to re-create the world from scratch.

TWO

The first garden was perfection. In it was the possibility not only for the purest fulfillment of the human race but for all of creation. It was meant to be a paradise, which is, in fact, no different from saying it was meant to be a garden — both words mean the same thing. Our word *paradise* comes from the Greek *paradeisos*, "garden," which comes from the Persian *pairidaeza*, an enclosed area, a wall around. Our English word *garden* finds its roots in the Old French *jardin* and the Old High German *gart*, both of which mean "enclosure." So a garden is a place that is set apart, a place with unique boundaries, an area that is protected and distinct from that which is without. It's meant to be something special.

Why did God need to set aside such a place? The world was newborn, unpolluted, an expression of his own spirit and just as vital and fresh: "God saw all that he had made, and it was very good" (Genesis 1:31). There was no death or destruction, no violence, no nature red in fang and claw. Humans did not kill and eat. God declares, "I give you every seed-bearing plant on the face of the whole earth and every tree that has fruit with seed in it. They will be yours for food" (1:29). The animals and birds did not kill and eat either: "And to all the beasts of the earth and all the birds of the air and all the creatures that move on the ground—everything that has the breath of life in it—I give every green plant for food" (1:30).

In a way, the entire earth seemed to be a garden, rescued from being formless and empty and dark, a vast wasteland enclosed and transformed in a matter of days, a planet with a wall around it that separated it from an environment in which humanity and other living creatures, plants, trees, and waters, could not survive. Earth itself became a garden in the galaxy.

Yet God still chose to plant a special garden amid all this goodness. God created the first person, then made the garden, and then placed the person in the garden to till it and look after it. A river had its source in Eden; it watered the garden and then split into four, only two rivers of which we can identify with certainty—the Tigris and the Euphrates.

It is in the garden that the first human experiences companionship with the creatures God has made, at least all those not confined to the seas: "The LORD God said, 'It is not good for the man to be alone. I will make a helper suitable for him.' Now the LORD God had formed out of the ground all the beasts of the field and all the birds of the air. He brought them to the man to see what he would name them" (2:18–19). The animals we enjoy as our companions today are a link to that Edenic experience, and we take as much enjoyment out of naming them as the first man presumably did. There was no fear or estrangement between the creatures of the air and the land and humanity at this point. They were all in it together, in this special garden within a garden, this goodness within goodness.

What sort of picture do we come up with for this first garden of all gardens? For many of us, a picture so extraordinary that Eden may seem like an illusion or a fantasy, something completely impossible, a place that could never exist except in our wildest dreams—no animal hurting another, no fighting, no bloodshed, no cruelty between man or beast in the whole wide world.

But perhaps we are supposed to see Eden in the light of the fantastic. After all, isn't this the work of the beyond-what-you-can-ask-or-imagine Gardener, a garden unrestricted by killing frosts or marauding tigers or global warming? Isn't Eden meant to represent an idyllic existence? Why else is a cow striking up a friendship with a bear, or a leopard lying down with a baby goat, or, for that matter, bats and dragonflies relaxing with gnats and mosquitoes? Isn't this the image of the perfect world Isaiah offers us (Isaiah 11)? Isn't this the image of the world as it was meant to be that Eden offers us? Surely the God of the platypus and ostrich and giraffe is a God of visions and dreams, and, if so, visions and dreams are an essential aspect of Eden and the Edenic. Whether we are capable of picturing it or not, everything was in the garden, including man and woman, and everything had a name, and it all fit.

THREE

A year after we were married, my wife and I moved to the city of Vancouver in Canada. We rented a basement suite that had a backyard patio. The small bit of yard beside the patio was no more than a tangle of tall grass and weeds and rocks. That spring, our landlords asked if we wanted to make a garden out of it, and Linda and I agreed to give it a try. I bought and devoured books on gardening. We learned how to double-dig so that the soil became a dark flour. We went down two feet or more. We yanked pop cans out of the ground. Plastic containers. Rusty spikes. I pried up boulders that I staggered around the patio with. My landlord hauled them across the street and dropped them into the waters of English Bay, where they were no longer covered by dirt but by the waves of the Pacific.

Once the soil was ready, we began to sprinkle tiny seeds into wide furrows. I remember thinking as the seeds fell (and I still think this every time I do it), "How can anything come out of these things? They are so small, and they look so dead." We wielded trowels and made a bed for tomato plants. Sunflower seeds went into the mix. The West Coast sun warmed the earth, water from the hose made rain.

Every morning before work we took a look. Nothing. Until the radishes came up all in a hurry, shouldering the earth aside and going for air. No radishes tasted better. Tomatoes rounded and ripened, though I did have to put a couple of dozen inside a dark cupboard to finish the process. The sunflowers must have thought they were from magic seeds. They grew and grew and grew up to the second floor and peeked inside our landlords' bedroom window. Both my wife and I were amazed; so were our landlords.

But as beautiful as it was to us, it was far from the paradise of Eden. Our garden didn't stay perfect. Worms ate into our radishes, and massive slugs invaded — some green, some black, some leopard-spotted, antennae up, sliding like aliens over the landscape. Cats stepped on everything, obviously not willing to relinquish a favorite trysting spot just because we had turned it into trim rows of vegetables and herbs. Still, the garden survived. And because it did, many an hour was spent with friends sitting in the backyard, talking and sipping lemonade and watching honeybees and monarch butterflies and the red robins that hopped between plants, cocked their heads, and cracked the earth with their beaks.

So we brought a garden into the world that had never existed before, just as Linda's parents had done years before in Nova Scotia.

The garden did not take over the world. It was just a very small and wonderfully new part of it. True to its name, the garden had its definite boundaries beyond which it could not go — a neighbor's fence, white patio stones, the back wall of the cedar house. Yet it brought peace and life and pleasure that were unique to that space. Where there had been chaos, it brought order; where things had been grim, it brought good cheer to a backyard that had been bleak and uninviting. This is what gardens are supposed to do. Even imperfect ones. And, as stories go, we know what happened to Eden's garden — it did not stay perfect either.

FOUR

Like watching the kind of film where all the beauty and happiness of the first hour disintegrates in the second, like a tragedy written by the Greek playwrights or by Shakespeare or by Job, like a bad dream that doesn't vanish when you wake up, Eden falls into ruins.

And with it falls everything. Indeed, here is where the headwaters of all human tragedy rise like a flood. Eden is the crux of the human dilemma: Why is a human existence that is so permeated with pleasure also so violated by suffering and death? A peaceful garden, a sweeping green that causes a rush to the heart, a golden light slanting over bright flowers and vivid leaves — every summer we experience this beauty. Why must it be so transient? Why is it impossible to stay in that garden, body and soul? Why is it only a glimpse, a moment, something given that swiftly becomes something lost? Why does the frost kill it? Why does the frost kill us?

In the middle of the garden, God has planted a choice. When all is said and done, it comes down to trust. Whose words matter? Whose voice? Man and woman go beyond God's words, and in so doing they go beyond God. They reach outside of the enclosure. They violate the embrace. Eden recurs throughout the history of the human race, and one of the ways in which it recurs is the choices made by generation after generation to go beyond the words of God and the garden wall. What God meant to be special is seen as a trap and a restriction, a denial of freedoms and rights and pleasures. The grass is lush on the other side. We're sure of it. The illusion is that outside of God and his words and his love is where a person finds what matters and what is sweet. The reality that is inevitably discovered is the same reality experienced by the man and the woman of Eden: Life outside the garden is no garden. It is exile.

The snake, forever marked as the one that starts the fall into ruin, is not in and of itself evil. We must remember that snakes, too, were part of the "very good-ness" of creation in Genesis 1. Man, *imago dei*, named it and was not estranged from it. Moses made a bronze snake at God's command and lifted it up on a pole so that anyone who had been bitten by a poisonous snake would recover (Numbers 21:8–9). This image of the snake on the pole, Nehushtan, remains today a symbol used by the medical profession to symbolize healing. It will also become an image of Christ and the cross, and thus a symbol of divine redemption: "Just as Moses lifted up the snake in the wilderness, so the Son of Man must be lifted up, that everyone who believes may have eternal life in him" (John 3:14–15 TNIV). Moreover, in that day when God's kingdom rules on earth, Isaiah tells us, "Infants will play near the hole of the cobra; young children will put their hands into the viper's nest" (Isaiah 11:8). When Eden returns to earth, the snake will be a friend of children, much as my son and daughter in their younger years lifted garter snakes from the creek behind our house, held them without fear, then returned them to the water gently and without hatred.

Clearly the snake or serpent in Eden is controlled by another force. God is squaring off against something more than snakes when he pronounces judgment within the garden: "I will put enmity between you and the woman, and between your offspring and hers; he will crush your head, and you will strike his heel" (Genesis 3:15). It is seen by many as a prophecy about Christ, that the adversary possessing the snake, a being later to be known as *Satan* (the name means "adversary" in Hebrew), will come into conflict with the Son of God, born to a woman, and will be defeated.

There is a curious passage in Ezekiel that is supposed to be about the majesty and arrogance of the king of Tyre but which, like the passage about the snake in the garden, seems to hold a double meaning:

> *"You were in Eden,*
> *   the garden of God....*
> *You were anointed as a guardian cherub,*
> *   for so I ordained you.*
> *You were on the holy mount of God;*
> *   you walked among the fiery stones.*
> *You were blameless in your ways*
> *   from the day you were created*
> *   till wickedness was found in you....*
> *So I drove you in disgrace from the mount of God,*
> *   and I expelled you, O guardian cherub,*
> *   from among the fiery stones."*

Ezekiel 28:13–16

The king of Tyre was no guardian cherub; he was never in

Eden. But another was — a cherub who fell from grace, a being of great pride and sparkling beauty — one who became for those who were in the image of God the voice of God.

Whether the man and woman fully realized the choice they were making, both of them were subordinating God's words to the words of another. There seemed to be a contradiction about what God had said or not said, and they chose to go with the one who voiced the contradiction. The man knew as well as the woman what kind of fruit he was biting into. He recognized it. He had seen it hanging from the tree in the middle of the garden — the tree of the knowledge of good and evil. It looked good. It tasted good. It was the thing to do. They could not only be in the image of God; they could be God. It seemed to be such a win-win deal. So they ate the fruit that gave the knowledge of good and evil, the fruit they thought would bring life to the fullest. And in so doing, they died.

The garden does not change; *they* change. Now they see nakedness. Now they hide their bodies. Now they hide from God. The Gardener, like any gardener, strolls about in his garden in the pleasant coolness of the evening of a warm day, examining his flowers and plants and shrubs, expecting his children who are made in his image to join him and enjoy the stroll with him, as they have always done. But the relationship is broken between parent and child. The freedom to be unafraid in God's presence and to be intimate with him is gone.

A moment later, we see that the relationship between humanity and the animal kingdom is also broken as first the woman accuses the snake and later as God slays an animal and uses the skin to clothe the woman and man (Genesis 3:13, 21). The first blood is shed on earth. It signifies an alienation of stunning magnitude between humanity and nature, as well as between humanity and God—even alienation between God and nature, since God never intended his living creatures to be killed for food or clothing. The break between humans and nature is reinforced by God's words to the man:

> *"Cursed is the ground because of you;*
>> *through painful toil you will eat of it*
>> *all the days of your life.*
> *It will produce thorns and thistles for you,*
>> *and you will eat the plants of the field.*
> *By the sweat of your brow*
>> *you will eat your food*
> *until you return to the ground."*

Genesis 3:17–19

There is even a chasm of pain that opens up between a woman and her own body, her own womb, in childbirth, and another that yawns wide and makes a woman subordinate to a man (3:16). The harmony of Eden is rapidly unraveling.

It gets worse. Man and woman are driven from the garden and denied immortality. God settles them to the east of Eden; but to ensure they do not desecrate the garden again or take what is not theirs to take, cherubim and a fiery sword that flashes and whirls block access to the tree of life. Humans will never be the gods they imagined they could be. Twice they are denied life by angels—once in the garden by a winged being disguised as a serpent, and again at the gate to the garden by an angelic being in full view with outspread wings and a sword that burns but is not consumed (Genesis 3:24). The Gardener is holy, and his garden is holy. But humans no longer are.

The tragedy will be compounded. There will be a firstborn, a son, and he will murder his younger brother, and human blood will soak into the dust from which humanity had been formed, mingling with the blood of animals killed not only for clothing and food but also for sacrifice (Genesis 4:1–10). Not only will murder continue, but pride and gloating in being a murderer (Genesis 4:23). Vengeance will come (4:24). Wickedness will increase from generation to generation until God will wish humans had never been born. The earth and the animals that were once in such unity in Eden are at war with each other and humanity—and when God punishes human wickedness, they will suffer along with women and men: "I will wipe from the face of the earth the human race I have created—and with them the animals, the birds and the creatures that move along the ground—for I regret that I have made them" (Genesis 6:7 TNIV).

But we take note that Evil is not birthed in Eden. It already exists. That is why there could be a tree that offered knowledge of it. God's idea was to form humanity in his image but to keep it safe from evil within the enclosure. Yet to stay within God's garden or not was, in the end, a choice that the first humans would be allowed to make; and in order for it to be a true choice, there needed to be a true option. The temptation was permitted, the Adversary allowed to be at large, "roaming through the earth and going back and forth in it," and be the tempter (Job 1:7). Human life—even more, the life of the entire earth—was meant to be other than it presently is. Genesis tells us the reason we no longer experience Eden is not because God forced a sinful humanity from the garden. We left it the moment we looked to someone other than God, and, the truth is, we continue to leave it, of our own free will, every time we look past him for life.

FIVE

When I was a boy, I grew up in a neighborhood where just about everyone had a garden, small or large, and not just of flowers. Raspberries, strawberries, carrots, tomatoes, potatoes, corn — you name it, our neighborhood grew it all. But there was one gardener who grew everything just a little bit sweeter, a little bit taller, a little bit better. He used trellises, he used poles, he used yards and yards of hose, he even used mirrors to reflect sunlight; and his garden filled the yard and touched the sky. My friends and I called him Mister Buon Giorno, Mister Good Morning, because he came from Italy and had such a warm, sunny, bright-new-morning disposition.

Every summer we all planted our gardens, and every summer his vegetables and fruit trees soared while ours merely inched their way above the soil line. And every harvest he gave extra apples and plums and potatoes away to others. We would often see him sitting in the middle of his garden in July, sipping a glass of water, totally relaxed, watching his plants thrive. I would often run down the back lane past his yard, and I always felt I was racing by some sort of jungle greenhouse without a roof or walls. His garden was like a great, green thumbprint among our lawns and houses, our concrete sidewalks and asphalt streets.

But the years went by, and in time he grew ill and could

not care for his garden as he once had—and it began to fall apart. Support poles broke, trellises sagged, trees withered, weeds spread. When he died, the garden died with him. His wife moved away, and the new owners cared nothing for what he had planted and tirelessly nurtured. They seeded the garden plot, and Mister Buon Giorno's Little Eden vanished under a thick carpet of Kentucky bluegrass. Yet even though all traces of its glory are gone, we never forget a garden like that or the man who created it. Like God, we look on such beauty and pronounce it good. It in turn plants something of itself in us that may take root and give life long after it has vanished from the earth.

If the biblical Eden is both a garden of birth and a garden of death, it is also a garden of grace. There are many gardens and many stories that follow Eden, and none of them would have been possible if God had not chosen to remain in relationship with his fallen creation—humans, birds, animals, fish and whales and giant squids, all flora and all fauna. Before Adam and Eve leave Eden, God permits the death of one of his animals so that they can be warm and adequately covered for the harsh existence ahead of them. The woman acknowledges that "with the help of the LORD I have brought forth a man" (Genesis 4:1). The ability to create human life reflects the work of God in creating human life. It is a great gift that is not destroyed by the fall. It survives. So does the coming together of man and woman (Genesis 2:24). One of the great blessings of the fall, in fact, is the development of sexuality—becoming one flesh. It is no longer simply for companionship that Adam and Eve enjoy intimacy, but in exile from the garden their relationship with one another becomes the means of procreation. When Adam is 130 years old, Eve births him "a son in his own likeness, in his own image" (Genesis 5:3) and names him Seth, which means "granted" (Genesis 4:25) — as if the wish of the human race to remain in existence and to keep the image of God that is their essence will be honored.

Perhaps one of the greatest surprises of the biblical story is that *imago dei* (the image of God in humans) is never extinguished. Even more surprisingly, despite the ups and downs and wicked twists of humanity, neither is God's desire to live in intimacy with men and women: "He will live with them. They will be his people, and God himself will be with them" (Revelation 21:3).

God, undying Gardener and Nurturer that he is, has not relinquished the dream and vision of another Eden where unity between himself and what he has made — all that he has made — will be restored. His quest for a second Eden is all-consuming — just as that same quest for paradise, for all the wrong turns it has taken, is all-consuming for the human heart. Not only will there be a garden at the end of the world, just as there was at the beginning; there will be many lesser gardens and oases along the way to refresh and reinvigorate the human spirit and to keep the hope alive. Eden is a symbol of what will be again and of what was always meant to be.

SIX

Between the first Eden and the second Eden hang the rest of the Bible and all of human history. We do not see this because we often do not see the significance of the first Eden to begin with. Genesis has become the battleground of creationists and evolutionists, of those who say it is legend and those who say it is literal. Some claim the truth within is the truth of a parable, while others claim it is the truth of a proposition — the facts presented are either true or false exactly as they stand. What is missed about Eden in particular is its essence: God created all life, and he wants to be intimate with it, close to it, especially with humanity, created so lovingly in his image. The thrust is that no matter who argues how it was done, *God* did it — not blind forces, not uninitiated chemical reactions, not a haphazard design with no intelligence behind it, not Nature without a Creator. Eden is a divine beginning. And to bring it back, which God fully intends, it will take nothing short of a divine restoration.

I wonder if too much emphasis is laid on the tragic end of Eden and too little on the beauty that existed at its beginning. Every good thing we experience is a reminder of the garden that was and the garden that will be again. Marriage, for example, is both an echo of the first Eden and the whisper of the coming Eden. Man and woman are united for the first time in the original Eden. The author of Genesis writes, "For this reason a man will leave his father and mother and be united to his wife, and they will become one flesh" (Genesis 2:24). After the fall, marriage continues to allow man and woman to experience something of the perfect unity that existed between them in the garden. In the second Eden, there will, at last, be true unity between them and their God. Jesus tells us there will no longer be marriage as we know it, but closeness between men and women will exist to a greater degree than was possible before — they will be like "the angels in heaven" (Matthew 22:30), experiencing intimacy with one another in a new kind of wholeness, as well as intimacy with God.

Even outside of the marriage relationship, friendship between humans is also both an echo of the unity that existed in the first Eden and the rumor of a second Eden in which all the good that happened in the first garden will happen again. So is friendship between animals and humans. So is the unlikely but not impossible friendship between typical enemies in the animal kingdom. So is harmony, rather than violence and exploitation, between humans and the natural environment.

Every newborn reminds us of our birth in Eden, of our birth after Eden and the continuation of the image of God in humans, and also of our new birth into the Eden that is to come, in which there will be no more death or suffering (Revelation 21:4). Everything that approaches the oneness and well-being and peace on earth God intended at the start and still intends is nothing short of Edenic. And all that is Edenic is the great desire of God.

SEVEN

Recently, my wife mentioned that the symbol for the Holy Spirit in the ancient Irish church was not the dove; it was the wild goose. This seems right and true. When the wild geese come north and bring spring with them, it is the Holy Spirit coming too, bringing Eden and all the gardens of Eden in his wings. The wild geese are the coming of God. And if these geese are a metaphor for divinity, Eden and gardens are no less metaphors for divinity and the human soul.

So Eden ought to be an encouragement to us. Its beauty is not lost. Like the coming of spring and the return of the wild geese, we will see it once more. We will experience it to the roots of our beings. It is a symbol of the sacred enclosure, and this sacred enclosure is the loving and encircling embrace of God. If we respond to God's love, we are within that embrace; we are within that garden. For the garden is not only a pleasure that will occur; it is a present reality of the human spirit for all who wish to live in relationship with their Creator and Redeemer.

Jesus walked through two gardens, Gethsemane and the Garden Tomb, to make the second Eden a powerful hope and to open the gate to an ever-present garden of the heart. Those who believe and pray — they know something of the garden of the heart, they know something of Eden. Those who worship the living God—they know something of the garden of the heart, they know something of Eden. Those who pick up their cross and follow Jesus, those who lay down their lives for the gospel, those who give cups of cold water to the little ones—they know something of the garden of the heart, they know something of Eden. As long as we live, those of us who believe have a garden of the heart. It never vanishes—no matter which weeds sprout in it or which thistles attempt to choke it. It is a planting of God. It is the circle of his arms. One day it will not only be within and uncluttered; it will be all around us, untainted and unending.

The garden of the heart is the one garden that cannot be lost, and it contains all the other gardens within its embrace. Truth be told, we lose some of the gardens in our lives, don't we? We have all known peace and pleasure, and we've all had our peace and pleasure shattered. We have experienced unity with others only to see that unity break apart. We have known intimacy with God, and we have lost intimacy with God. Relationships with friends, with children, marriages, we have seen all of this wonder come to an end in our lives or in the lives of others. We have known Eden, and we have known what it is to be outside of Eden, barred from its peace. We have suffered. We have wept. We have felt we had nothing to live for.

Yet we know something of what we have lost. We have experienced bits and pieces of what is good and right, and we know good and right exist. Even if it seems we cannot find it again—no matter how hard we try or how hard we pray—we know it is there. We were in Eden once, if only for a few moments or hours or years. Yesterday we were there. The gardens of the

Bible tell us we will come back inside it again. The gardens we plant with our minds and our hands tell us. The garden of the heart tells us. One day, Eden will fill our souls, fill all our senses, fill our entire world.

I once lost a dog that had been my constant companion for almost fifteen years. I went with him and his mate on well over ten thousand walks and traveled literally over ten thousand miles through cities and forests and mountain ranges and along the shores of the sea. In all moods I walked, whether I was living or dead, up or down, close to God or far away, hopeful or fearful. I talked to that dog constantly. But our real communication was done with touch — through the emotions I voiced or did not voice, in silence as I lay beside him, or the long looks into the eyes. When he died, pain roared through me like a storm surge. I felt I had been violated and beaten and left in a ditch of stones. I had known friendship with another creature. I had known a harmony that was meant to exist. I had known a great happiness that made me feel like a nine-year-old boy. And I had lost it all and lost him.

A few hours after he died, I went to a window in my house and looked out, as I had looked out hundreds of times. I knew why I was there. I was hoping to see him. I was hoping I had somehow been mistaken and that he was still alive. I stood there a long time, praying and waiting. A voice inside me asked, "What are you looking for, Murray?" And I answered without thinking, "I am looking for Eden."

What I experienced with Yukon had been Edenic. Inside, I had known this. I had relished every minute of the relationship, all the months, all the days. How many years had I expected it to continue? Sixteen? Seventeen? Twenty? I knew the answer to that as well: forever.

We lose parents. We lose children. We lose brides and bridegrooms. We lose animal companions. We lose beautiful vistas and beautiful dreams. We even lose ourselves. Yet we know Eden when we see it, even if sometimes we see it after it is over; and that sense of place, that sense of paradise gained and paradise lost, that sense of grief, to me is a proof of the truth of the story. And if the first story is true, all of the other stories caught up in it must be also. This is the hope the first garden gives us. That the stories of God are the true stories of the world and that he will plant another garden for us, another Eden in the east, and put us in it.

PART TWO

En Gedi
The GARDEN *of* LOVE

My lover is to me a cluster of henna blossoms
from the vineyards of En Gedi.
Song of Songs 1:14

ONE

The green army truck bounced and jolted its way across the hot desert. Looking out, I saw yellow and purple mountains bristling with boulders, and crags standing defiantly under the hammer blows of the scorching sun. A friend kept banging his shoulder against mine as the truck lurched over rock and stone. We sat with ten others on a long wooden bench bolted to the bed of the truck, facing more of our friends who were sitting on the bench across from us.

Strong, dark canvas that stretched over the back of the truck protected us from the blazing sky. But sweat still glistened on my hands and face, and fine dust spun golden in the air and filled my nostrils. Two men with Uzi submachine guns sat at the end of each bench and leaned their heads out of the opening, squinting. Oded, with his thick black curls, looked at us and shrugged. "Camels or trucks, a desert is still a desert," he said. "Heat, dust, stones. What can you do? But we are very close now."

Ten minutes more of jostling, and then the truck rolled to a stop. We climbed out and stretched and looked around. More desert. More heat. But now a sheet of blue water.

"Good," I said. "We can swim and cool off in the water."

"Sure," grinned Oded, slinging his Uzi. "You can try. But you'll bob like a cork. It's the Dead Sea."

There was only one person in the water. A man floated calmly on his back, perfectly immobile, reading a newspaper as if he were sitting on a couch in his living room. I'm not sure how he did that because after I jumped in, my body always wanted to turn upside down. We ran splashing into the water and then ran splashing out. The salt and other chemicals burned into any open cut or scratch like fire — the Dead Sea is nine times saltier than the Mediterranean Sea. A few minutes in the open air evaporated the water but left the salt behind like long threads of white all over my body. My cuts and nicks shrieked for relief.

"Come," said Oded, "we'll go to a better place."

The group of us came from all over the world. We had come to Israel to work on a kibbutz, a kind of communal settlement, and most of us had spent the fall picking oranges and grapefruit or working with beef cattle. At various times I and the others had hitchhiked into Jerusalem and Tel Aviv or down to Eilat and the Red Sea. This trip in the army truck had been arranged by the kibbutz to help us see more of the desert.

Thankfully, the next drive was much shorter. It brought us to the beautiful waters that would wash both salt and pain from my skin. I spent about a half hour swimming and diving in a large pool at the foot of limestone cliffs. It was surrounded by palms and ferns and speckled with sunlight that made its way through the greenery. While I enjoyed this first pool, almost everyone else had climbed up the cliffs to look at the other pools. When I finally joined them, I was astonished at what I saw. Water was racing down the rock wall and splashing into a pool cupped in the basin of a limestone ledge. Water would pour out of this pool and drop twenty or thirty feet into another pool. This water would in turn pour down into yet another pool, and so on all the way to the bottom. My friends were sliding on their backsides on the smooth limestone and falling with the rush of water from pool to pool. I leaped in, the warm water spraying my face and arms as I slid down from level to level, plunging under the surface of each pool, surfacing and sliding down again to burst into the next. Anyone who has been to these waterfalls and pools will know that calling them a piece of paradise is not an exaggeration. The name of the oasis is En Gedi, the Fountain of the Young Goats.

It's like a large garden. But there is far more to it than the balsam trees and palms and plants that grow there in profusion. There are many beautiful birds, for one thing. And animals. Oded quietly pointed out two deerlike animals as they grazed on cliffs above us. They were really more gazelle than deer, I guess, lifting their heads and horns when they spotted us, watching, then turning and bounding through the tall ferns.

Scattered throughout the oasis were numerous caves. People had once lived in them — archaeologists have found their pottery as well as many other items. In fact, David once hid in these caves from the pursuit of King Saul: "After Saul returned from pursuing the Philistines, he was told, 'David is in the Desert of En Gedi'" (1 Samuel 24:1). It was at this time that David cut off a corner of Saul's robe while Saul was relieving himself in one of the caves (1 Samuel 24:4). David and his men — numbered at

600 in the biblical text—remained out of sight at En Gedi until the death of Samuel the prophet. No doubt the fresh water, fruit, and wild game, not to mention the sheer beauty of the place, helped compensate for the emotional drain and rigors of living the life of a fugitive.

TWO

Isn't it strange that the very ground God cursed at Eden, strewing it with thistles and thorns, has become a source of such pleasure to gardeners the world over? Sweat on the brow there is, but this sweat is simply considered part of the good sensation of working the land, a benefit that goes along with the cultivation of honeysuckle or corn or a patch of turnips. It's as if God granted this grace also, that those who would garden would grow to love gardening, and in that love the curse would become unstrung, in a way, and the soil yield something of the rapture of Eden.

The love of gardening was not only part of Linda's family but seems to be part of my family's DNA as well. Dad and Mom grew flowers and vegetables, and so did most of my aunts and uncles. I don't know if the vegetable gardens were a holdover of the sentiment from the Depression in the 1930s, when you grew as much of your own food as you could, or a result of the rationing of the Second World War, when fresh produce was often hard to come by. But I have strong memories of forests of dark-green spinach and the red-veined leaves of beets bending in a summer breeze, of corn stalks like a wall of jungle bamboo, of bushes drooping with pea pods—not just at my own home but at all my relatives' homes.

I recall one aunt who was always slipping a pair of scissors out of her purse and secretly snipping cuttings from flower beds that surrounded government buildings in town so she could propagate the plants for her own garden. Dill and heads of lettuce and radishes and black earth and blue-sky heat are associated in my mind with the numerous religious figurines and dark-eyed icons of Jesus and Mary in this aunt's house: Mary stares at me, Jesus stares at me—eyes from a world that is not this world. A jumble of other images of life and death and eternity come to mind also: my aunt's father lies in an open coffin in a black-and-white photograph framed on a bedroom wall; crucifixes and brown-potted geraniums on window sills mingle with doilies and shafts of light; a heap of orange carrots on the kitchen table brings the smell of earth indoors, as well as the sharpness of broken green where their tops have been twisted off.

On my father's side, the family came from Galicia or west Ukraine, and the long and deep winding syllables of Ukrainian were part of the love language of their gardens. My mother's line was mostly German, though given the fluid borders in the nineteenth century, Mom said it was likely we had French and Swiss in us too. But the German blood was enough for an angry mob of Canadians to paint crosses on my grandfather's barn and then burn it to the ground during the First World War. After seeking refuge in a nearby city, he decided to grow a garden.

He was not a kind or loving man, as I remember him, and the stories of his rages are part of the family legend. Perhaps whatever love he had went into the garden. It was not large, but it was full. Everything grew there behind the small, red-shingle house, including cabbages and onions and a thick-trunked apple tree. The tree shed its grace over everyone who came into the backyard, including Grandfather—white blossoms in the spring, pale yellow apples in the late summer and fall. There he is, short and thin, suspenders keeping his pants up, walking up and down the planks he had placed between the rows of vegetables, some sort of long trowel in one hand, a bunch of radishes he has just pulled up in the other.

It sounds naive, but I don't remember anyone (including my grandfather) ever fighting in the gardens of my family. They must have been magical regions in which some sort of special truce was in effect. People grunted and pointed and thrashed at Scotch thistles with hoes and muttered about potato beetles, but in the end the gardens were simply good places to be. Insects buzzed, sun was like syrup, the air was glossy—it was all about being alive and feeling a kind of forever in your blood. Grandfather smelled like apples and dirt, my aunt like dill and dirt, my dad like potatoes and dirt. It's not too much of a stretch to say that in my family, love smelled like a metal watering can and dirt.

I've dug gardens in numerous locations around the world. In Canada, not only for my mother and father but later for myself and my wife and my children. In the United States, pulling up weeds in California and hoeing the soil and having to fight off a dangerous black widow spider in the process. In Israel, planting roses and bushes and trees, placing flowers by the graves of the dead, coaxing flowers alongside the houses of the living. In all of those places I felt good after spending hours in the soil and under the sun, with my lungs full of the sweet, good scent of an air that also spent time with growing things.

Love is easy in a garden. Even if the garden is only growing horseradish and Brussels sprouts. That must be another smudge of Eden. A rose garden — or any garden — is a place of romance, and you can set up tables and chairs, sip cool drinks, and stare into your lover's eyes. But the romance can be as much between you and the butterflies and bees and borage as between you and your lover. It can be a place for the romance of memory or the romance of what is not yet. It can be a place where your romantic interest is God. That is the thing about a garden — the surreal swiftly mixes with the real, and a great deal is possible that outside the garden was impossible.

We have a garden in our backyard. I have asked my wife to sit there with me a number of times. You talk differently in a garden. The flowers and nuthatches and the fall of moonlight or sunshine soften your words and thoughts. Romeo and Juliet declared their love for each other in the garden outside the walls of her house. Gardens are meant to be places for such declarations.

THREE

Woman completed what was lacking in the paradise of Eden. Man had companionship with all the living creatures, but it was not enough. There was an aspect of relationship missing. Yes, there was God, and man was, after all, made in God's image. There was the very earth that Adam worked, and a pleasant work it was early on, not a drudgery to be cursed. There were the birds lighting on his hands and arms and at his feet, the animals standing at his side or gazing calmly into his eyes. Yet something unmade still needed to be made.

Out of the dust of man, as man slept his deep sleep — just as the earth slept before the days of creation — God formed woman, *imago dei* out of *imago dei*. Man recognized immediately the finality of this act of God. This was the true companion, a soul friend (an *anamchara*, as the ancient Irish church put it) — one human spirit to encourage and guide another. The possibility of relationship as full and rounded as the earth itself seemed to be ensured — human to human, human to creation, human to all living creatures, human to God. All was now as it should be. There was no alienation. Naked as newborn infants, the man and woman lived as one in the garden, comfortable, at peace, stroking wolf and lamb alike, strolling with God among ferns and date palms, the river glinting through the rosebushes and tall, green reeds. All innocence, all childlike, at play in a field God had embraced, a spaciousness within a spaciousness, a place where the boundaries secured full life and full freedom — a "keeping in" that denied nothing except that which came only to steal, kill, and destroy (John 10:10). The first garden of all peoples and all nations was well named — *Eden*, Hebrew for "a place of pleasure."

You may have noticed that the man and woman in Eden do not have personal names until after their alienation from God. The curse has been pronounced. They are on the verge of being expelled from the garden when suddenly, in Genesis 3:20, the man names his wife Eve, and in 4:25, we are told the man's name is Adam (some translations call him Adam prior to this verse).* Eve, in Hebrew, means "living," or "to live." Adam is simply the same Hebrew word used for man from the beginning of Genesis. There is a special grace in this post-alienation naming. Banished, cursed, they are not statistics with God, not nameless and faceless and doomed to wander the earth as unknowns. They are named because *they are known*, and God will remember them. By the same token, their anonymity in Eden does not make them statistics there either. The lack of personal names lends a universality to the story. They are not Adam and Eve; they are everyone.

This same way of talking about gardens and the people God puts in them is carried over into the Bible's second garden (in the Song of Songs). Once again, the woman is not named; neither is the man. They could be anyone. They are simply "the bride and

---

* See Genesis 2:20; 3:17, 21.

the bridegroom," or "the beloved and her lover." Eugene Peterson, in *The Message*, designates them as "The Woman and The Man." They are any of us; they are all of us. This second garden is also a garden of humanity.

This garden could have been centered on any number of themes—justice, for instance, or eternity or the goodness of God or heaven. In fact, the theme is simply *love*. And by being love, in some way it encompasses all the themes I've just mentioned and much more. As a matter of fact, once God and love are put into the same mix, is there anything in heaven or earth that is not affected?

There are many gardens in the Song of Songs. The bride is a garden: "You are a garden locked up, my sister, my bride; you are a spring enclosed, a sealed fountain" (Song 4:12). The bridegroom is a garden: "My lover," cries the bride, "is to me a cluster of henna blossoms .... Like an apple tree among the trees of the forest is my lover among the young men. I delight to sit in his shade, and his fruit is sweet to my taste" (1:14; 2:3).

The bride and bridegroom enjoy their love for one another in garden settings: "He has taken me into the wine-garden and given me loving glances.... Let us go early to the vineyards and see if the vine has budded or its blossom opened, or if the pomegranates are in flower. There I shall give you my love, when the mandrakes yield their perfume" (2:4; 7:12–13 REB).

There is no portion of the Bible more saturated in garden imagery than the Song of Songs, no section in Scripture where the senses of smell and sight and taste are so powerfully evoked, nowhere among the words of God where sensuality and sexuality are so intricately and beautifully entwined with the radiance of divinity.

Very little is made of the Song of Songs by Christians today. Indeed, very little has been made of it for the past two hundred years. But the vast majority of Christians, over the span of nearly two thousand years, have found the book rich in allegory. The bride is the church pining after the love of the Savior, Jesus Christ. Or the bride is just one person longing for the presence of God. The bridegroom is Christ, passionate for his church or passionate for one woman or one man. The bridegroom is God the Creator, aching to be close to his people again, intense in his desire to be among the colors and scents of Eden with the humans he loves. Early in Christianity, the book (it is really a cluster of love poems) was interpreted in this fashion, following after Jewish allegory, which saw it as describing the love between Israel and God. Hippolytus, Origen, and Gregory of Nyssa all walked this path. So did Bernard of Clairvaux in the Middle Ages. So did the English Puritans of the seventeenth century. "Every Christian soul is the spouse of Christ," wrote Richard Sibbes, "as the whole church is."*

Nowadays, the Song of Songs is used to argue that God made sex and made it to be enjoyed; that Christian spirituality has a romantic twist that enthusiastically celebrates the pleasure of human sexuality; that the love between a bride and bridegroom —in other words, the love between a wife and her husband—is the God-made place to enjoy the God-made ecstasy of two

---

* A. B. Grosart, ed., *The Complete Works of Richard Sibbes* (Edinburgh: James Nichol, 1862), 2:202.

becoming one physically (not just emotionally and spiritually), an ecstasy that began in Eden, before the temptation and before the fall, when Eve and Adam became one flesh (Genesis 2:24). If this emphasis is a corrective to the suppression of the holy excitement of sex in marriage that blighted Christians in other generations, it is a welcome realignment of humanity with divinity.

I used generous amounts of the Song of Songs, in all its sparkling explicitness, when I wrote and spoke my own marriage vows, and later persuaded a friend to do the same when I was his best man. But there is surely more to the Song of Songs than just this. For it is the one garden that forges a link between disaster and salvation, between the fall of Eden and the redemption of Gethsemane. We can see that it is a celebration of "becoming one flesh" that springs up between husband and wife. But can we see, as other generations saw, that it is also a celebration of the "becoming one spirit" that ought to exist between humanity and God? If we look closely at this garden, we will catch a glimpse, perhaps more, of Eden-that-was and Eden-that-will-be. In fact, all gardens are in this garden. All humanity and all divinity. It is a mosaic of the five gardens and excludes nothing. What is unquestionably a human romance is also the romance of God. What else could the garden of love be if God is love?

FOUR

Many of the gardens in the Song of Songs are mystical or sexual or simply unnamed. En Gedi is the one we can identify, the one we can walk or drive to. It is the one we can touch with our fingertips. "My lover is to me," the bride smiles, "a cluster of henna blossoms from the vineyards of En Gedi" (1:14). All around En Gedi are the harsh sands of the Judean Desert. August temperatures can reach 120 degrees Fahrenheit (49 degrees Celsius). Rainfall is scant, only an inch or two a year on average. Just a little over ten miles to the south is the ancient hilltop fortress of Masada, where Jewish forces held out against Flavius Silva and the Roman Tenth Legion in AD 72 and 73. A mile to the west is the Dead Sea, the lowest point on the earth's surface at 1,310 feet below sea level. En Gedi itself is 984 feet below sea level, but it is still almost 400 feet above the Dead Sea. This permits the water I swam in to cascade down cliffs and bring life to a plain about a mile long and half a mile wide.

In the time of the Song of Songs, it was one of the world's most famous gardens. Wonderful things grew here — all the more wonderful because scarcely anywhere in the vast region surrounding En Gedi is there fertile land. The lushness of En Gedi is a surprise. Thousands of years ago, melons were cultivated here, as was sugarcane. There were vineyards and palm trees and balsam, pomegranates and other fruits, aromatic plants, grasses for wildlife that lived in or near the oasis. It really was a reminder of the Garden of Eden.

So En Gedi is the rose of God in the middle of the Judean wilderness. It serves the same function in Scripture, poised as it is between Eden and Gethsemane. Humanity is banished. Although there is love from the hand of God—rainfall, good harvests, seasons of peace between seasons of war, healing herbs for illness and plagues, the birth of children and grandchildren, prophets and priests of goodwill—the human race is still alienated from their Father and Creator, still in a spiritual wilderness, still battling spiritual thistles and thorns, still haunted by the relentless visage of death. There is only this one oasis, one respite, amid the waves of heat and the dry streambeds and the miles of barren sand.

The heart of this garden is found in the Song of Songs' last group of poems:

> *Love is invincible facing danger and death.*
> *Passion laughs at the terrors of hell.*
> *The fire of love stops at nothing—*
> *it sweeps everything before it.*
> *Flood waters can't drown love,*
> *torrents of rain can't put it out.*
> *Love can't be bought, love can't be sold—*
> *it's not to be found in the marketplace.*
>
> Song 8:6–7 MSG

Love is the equal of death in any contest. It is not inferior.

Its power is frightening. Its desire to hold on to and protect the one loved is fierce, is fire, is God's fire. This fire cannot be extinguished.

Who could guess that something so gentle and beautiful could be so volcanic and overwhelming? But anyone who has loved another knows the truth of this poetry. Do we also know that this is the love of God for his people and his world? Do we know how hot the fire blazes in his heart? Do we know that his love rises like a Matterhorn of killing flame against the ice flood of evil and death?

No romantic thriller on earth, no matter how well written or cleverly plotted, can come close to the intensity and ferocity of a God whose love for another is unimpeded by an obstacle of any kind.

FIVE

The first place my wife and I lived after we were married was a farmhouse in the Annapolis Valley of Nova Scotia. This is a beautiful area of thriving apple orchards and long, rolling fields of crops, including acres of strawberry plants that glitter red in spring and summer. Every window you looked out of in the old farmhouse was like a framed oil painting of rich land and vibrant sky. There couldn't have been a more romantic location for newlyweds.

Our landlords lived in their area of the farmhouse just beside us. They loved to plant gardens nearly as much as they loved each other. In April and May, they broke out the tools and began to turn the soil. These were not small gardens they created. It was a lot of work—and they were both in their seventies. But they did it together, and they didn't want any help. It was their way of spending time with one another. They told us they had done this for their entire married life. Heat did not stop them; neither did stubborn clods of earth or lack of rain or tired bodies.

One afternoon, I looked out the window and watched them seeding. Sun pounded on his back. She fussed around with labels and sticks at the edge of each row. At one point they sat down together to drink the iced tea she had prepared. They looked out over the large garden, and I could see their lips moving in conversation. Then, for a few minutes, she simply leaned her head on his shoulder as young lovers might. They are both gone now, but this is the way I remember them. Nothing stopped their gardening. Nothing stopped their love for each other.

The love between God and his people has that same passion and resiliency. The bride speaks first in the Song of Songs, the person loved by God. It's easy enough to trace how the bride has become an allegory for God's people. In Hosea, the imagery of romance is clear, as God says this about Israel:

> *"Therefore I am now going to allure her;*
> *I will lead her into the desert*
> *and speak tenderly to her ...*
>
> *"In that day," declares the LORD,*
> *"you will call me 'my husband' ....*
> *I will betroth you to me forever;*
> *I will betroth you in righteousness and justice,*
> *in love and compassion.*
> *I will betroth you in faithfulness,*
> *and you will acknowledge the LORD."*
>
> Hosea 2:14, 16, 19–20

Eugene Peterson puts it this way:

> *And now, here's what I'm going to do:*
> *I'm going to start all over again.*
> *I'm taking her back out into the wilderness*
> *where we had our first date, and I'll court her....*

"At that time"—this is GOD's Message still—
  "you'll address me, 'Dear husband!' . . .
And then I'll marry you for good—forever!
  I'll marry you true and proper, in love and tenderness.
  Yes, I'll marry you and neither leave you nor let you go.
  You'll know me, GOD, for who I really am."

                              Hosea 2:14, 15, 19–20 MSG

Jeremiah uses the same imagery of romance—imagery given to him by God (as Hosea's was). He writes, "This is what the LORD says: 'I remember the devotion of your youth, how as a bride you loved me and followed me through the wilderness, through a land not sown'" (Jeremiah 2:2).

When John the Baptist's disciples express jealousy about the crowds now running after Jesus, John alludes to a special relationship between the Messiah and his people. He tells them the people belong to the Messiah, not to him, and he uses the imagery of marriage and the Song of Songs to do it:

> "You yourselves can testify that I said, 'I am not the Messiah but am sent ahead of him.' The bride belongs to the bridegroom. The friend who attends the bridegroom waits and listens for him, and is full of joy when he hears the bridegroom's voice. That joy is mine, and it is now complete."

                              John 3:28–29 TNIV

This biblical emphasis—set out by Hosea and Jeremiah and continued in John's description of the relationship between Jesus and his people—that God's people are his bride or wife is picked up by Paul in his second letter to the church at Corinth: "I am jealous for you," he writes, "with a godly jealousy. I promised you to one husband, to Christ, so that I might present you as a pure virgin to him" (2 Corinthians 11:2).

Paul develops this theme further in his letter to the Ephesians:

> Husbands, love your wives, just as Christ loved the church and gave himself up for her to make her holy, cleansing her by the washing with water through the word, and to present her to himself as a radiant church, without stain or wrinkle or any other blemish, but holy and blameless.... He who loves his wife loves himself. After all, people have never hated their own bodies, but they feed and care for them, just as Christ does the church — for we are members of his body. "For this reason a man will leave his father and mother and be united to his wife, and the two will become one flesh." This is a profound mystery — but I am talking about Christ and the church.
>
> Ephesians 5:25 – 32 TNIV

What Paul unpacks here is astounding. The words as old as Eden, "A man will leave his father and mother and be united to his wife, and the two will become one flesh," are not simply about human marriage but about the marriage of Christ and his people, his church. It is only a natural progression then for the word of God to consummate its message in a Bach-like crescendo with the vibrant marriage imagery of the Revelation to John:

"The wedding of the Lamb has come,
     and his bride has made herself ready,
Fine linen, bright and clean,
     was given her to wear."

(Fine linen stands for the righteous acts of the saints.)

Then the angel said to me, "Write: 'Blessed are those who are invited to the wedding supper of the Lamb!' "

Revelation 19:7 – 9

I saw the Holy City, the new Jerusalem, coming down out of heaven from God, prepared as a bride beautifully dressed for her husband. And I heard a loud voice from the throne saying, "Look! God's dwelling place is now among the people, and he will dwell with them. They will be his people, and God himself will be with them and be their God."

Revelation 21:2 – 3 TNIV

One of the seven angels who had the seven bowls full of the seven last plagues came and said to me, "Come, I will show you the bride, the wife of the Lamb." And he carried me away in the Spirit to a mountain great and high, and showed me the Holy City, Jerusalem, coming down out of heaven from God. It shone with the glory of God, and its brilliance was like that of a very precious jewel, like a jasper, clear as crystal.

Revelation 21:9 – 11

It's obvious. The people of God are his bride, and his wife his church, believers from all nations, races, and generations. He will be joined to these believers, united as intimately as a husband to his wife. From Genesis to Revelation, this is God's overriding concern — to be married to the one he adores and, in doing so, to create a whole new world. The prince marries the princess, and they live happily ever after — this time it's for real. The princess was often a scruffy and unfaithful bride-to-be. No matter. The love of the prince has fought through hell for her, and his kiss transforms her from rags to riches. She will be in white, a virgin, unspoiled, as radiant as a million diamonds, luminous with the glory of God. It is the greatest love story ever told.

SIX

I wonder if you've ever felt the love of God as a powerful, unmistakable force in your life. I wonder if you've ever had an experience of his love that is so overwhelming you sense you could die at that moment and not feel any shock or fear. I have had such touches of his grace a few times, and I remember them all. One of them happened in a garden; in fact, it happened in the garden of my wife's parents, the garden by the sea.

We were visiting them on a summer holiday. Nova Scotia is always wonderful, but the summer with its white and blue waves and its beaches of golden or red sand, sailboats drifting like bright clouds over the rim of the sea—all this makes it a land of magic. That summer, however, there were a lot of storms, a lot of cloud cover—day after miserable day—and it started to get to me. I am one of those people who don't do well in cloudy climates. Too much of the gray, and I begin to feel hemmed in and trapped, claustrophobic. Under severe circumstances, I can even get frightening panic attacks in which I feel like there's no way out.

As grim day followed grim day, the darkness grew inside me until it felt like it was going to swallow me. I told my wife I was giving serious thought to heading back home early without her and the kids, just to get out of the gloom before I really got depressed. It would be a disappointment for all of us, but I was feeling so lousy I didn't know what else to do. The forecast gave no hope for a respite. In fact, I wasn't even sure how I'd get through the last few days before I could pick up a flight back west.

We went to a dinner theatre presentation in Halifax with my wife's jovial family of Maritimers one evening. I tried to put up a brave front and join in the boisterous party spirit, but the fog and cloud was thick and the night thicker, and I felt awful inside. When it came time to go home, I dreaded the thought of trying to get to sleep with such heaviness on me and such feelings of despair. I knew that when this kind of weather system moves in, especially when it is bolstered by a spent hurricane lumbering up the eastern coastline of the United States like this one was, we were going to be socked in for days with no chance of a break in the weather. There was no use hoping otherwise—that's just the way the climate worked here. I prayed, of course, but more along the lines of asking for the strength to endure than for any miraculous parting of the clouds and mist.

We rolled into the driveway, and I got out of the car with my heart locked solid in my boots. How was I going to get through the night when my whole body was on the verge of despair? I glanced up at the leaden banks of fog that smothered the night sky and got one of the big shocks of my life. The sky was crystal clear.

"That's unusual," someone said and went into the house. It made no difference to them whether the sky was gray or green or crystal clear. But to me, it was life.

I ran into the backyard that sloped down to the cove. Not only was the sky clear; it was thick with stars—and I mean thick—scarcely a patch of black between the clusters of glittering white. It was the kind of night sky I was used to seeing in the mountains, when the Milky Way is a bright stream and the stars are crushed glass on black cloth. I had never seen anything like it at sea level. The whole night throbbed with the vitality of the galaxies.

I grabbed a chair and plunked it down by the garden. Rosebushes brushed my shoulder. My wife visited with me for a while, delighted at how the opening up of the night had opened me up inside, then she headed for bed. But I stayed up half the night, gazing and gazing at the stars, brimming with gratitude and praise, thanking God with every fiber of my being.

You must understand that for me it was more than seeing the flashing constellations or the miles of shimmering sea. It was as if I could see the face of God beaming down at me through the orbs of fire strewn from one end of my vision to another. I conversed with him as I looked at the pulsing lights. I felt my soul filling with joy and ecstasy and did not care if I died by the garden under that good night because I had absolutely no fear, no panic, no dread. I felt so close to God and his love. Nothing came between us in those hours. The sky was a silver rose of his passion for me unfolding against the darkness. It was one of the most astounding spiritual experiences of my life.

By the time I went to bed, at three or four in the morning, fog banks had begun to drift in again. It didn't matter. God and all his burning stars and suns were inside me, sealed with his kisses of fire. Although the next day was overcast, it did not affect me—I was still glowing inside from the night before. In fact, the feeling in my heart and mind of his blazing love never left me during my remaining days in Nova Scotia. I never took an early flight home. I didn't have to. The fear was gone. Light surged up in me, and I laughed in freedom and pleasure. I was in love. And someone greater than the sum of my fears loved me. This is how God romances his bride; this is how he takes in his arms the men and women he loves and hugs them fiercely and rescues them from a cruel and impenetrable darkness.

The Song of Songs, or Canticles (from the Latin *canere*, "to sing") is this entire epic romance between us and God neatly fitted into one love song. The bride sets it off by expressing her longing for the love of her lover: "Let him kiss me with the kisses of his mouth" (Song 1:2). Her companions affirm the love they see between the two: "We rejoice and delight in you" (1:4). Yet the bride feels insecure about the way she looks (she is dark because she has been burnt by the sun) and about her past (her brothers were unhappy with her and sent her to watch over the vineyards, but she neglected to watch over her own vineyard; 1:6). This is not an issue for the bridegroom. He loves her regardless: "How beautiful you are, my darling! Oh, how beautiful! Your eyes are doves.... Like a lily among thorns is my darling among the maidens" (1:15; 2:2). God takes his people as they are, sees their true beauty despite outward appearances and circumstances, and sweeps them up in the shining romance of divine love.

In Eden, the fruit left a bitter taste in the mouth of the

human race. But in this garden, God the lover is the tree, an apple tree. He provides coolness from life's heat, and the fruit he offers is good: "Like an apple tree among the trees of the forest is my lover among the young men. I delight to sit in his shade, and his fruit is sweet to my taste" (2:3).

It is God the lover who takes the initiative again and again. He brings his bride, his people, into the wine-garden, strengthens his people with raisins, refreshes them with apples—his own spiritual fruit—pillows them with his left arm, embraces them with his right (2:4–6). He races over high mountain barriers to be with them, comes in the spring when life is released from winter's grip, and invites his people to drop everything and join him (2:8–13). In a love song brimming with allegory, it is not far-fetched to point out that, according to Jewish tradition, the Messiah would come to rescue his people at Passover, in the spring. And it was at Passover time, in the Middle-Eastern spring, that Jesus the Messiah died for his people.

The next event that occurs in the Song of Songs is a shadow passing over the sun that brings warmth and light to the garden. The bride is separated from her lover. "All night long on my bed I looked for the one my heart loves; I looked for him but did not find him" (3:1). What has separated them? We don't know, but the bride's anguish is real. She runs into the streets and hunts for her lover throughout the city. She is no longer in the garden of love. Instead of henna blossoms, she has stone walls; instead of grass, cold paving stones; instead of apple trees, tall and dark buildings. The night watchmen find her, obviously distraught, and she blurts out, "Have you seen the one my heart loves?" (3:3)

No sooner does she ask this than her lover appears: "Scarcely had I passed them when I found the one my heart loves. I held him and would not let him go" (3:4).

Sometimes, for reasons that are not always clear, a sense of distance comes between two people in love. In Christianity, we speak about a dark night of the soul—it's an experience mirrored in this passage. God is nowhere to be found. Our worship is flat, our prayers lifeless. We feel as though the one we love has left us and is not coming back. We get desperate for him. We read books on spirituality, attend conferences, undergo counseling. *God is gone. I do not feel his presence. What have I done to displease him? Why has he abandoned me?* Even to strangers we go for help, such as the night watchmen, people we would not expect to care for our romantic concerns. We humiliate ourselves. "Have you seen the One I love?" we demand of those least involved in our lives.

This is how frantic we can get if we feel that our spiritual ardor is dead and the God we love has vanished—and with him all that we live for. This experience is common to Christians from all time periods and all denominations. Nearly two thousand years of Christian literature wrestle with the phenomenon. Even Jesus knew the separation many of us have felt—and to a far greater degree, for he was torn apart not only from God the Father but, as God incarnate, in some way from his very self—"My God, My God, why have you forsaken me?" (Matthew 27:46). He knows the misery we know; he suffers as we suffer—and even more so. When we come to him in pain, we do not come to a God distant and aloof from our agony.

Yet a positive comes out of this painful night. The bride realizes more strongly than before that her lover really is her true love. And she immediately seeks to renew their intimacy: "I held him and would not let him go till I had brought him to my mother's house, to the room of the one who conceived me" (3:4). Christians who find their faith renewed and their spiritual love rekindled know this feeling. Suddenly we can't get enough of the Bible or prayer or worship; we can't wait to get alone with God. We crave intimacy. We are on fire for it. The intensity of these feelings makes it clear why Paul suggests that marriage and sexual love are metaphors for the union and intimacy between God and the people who love and worship him.

As often happens, gloom dispersed — mentally, spiritually, and physically — brings on a brighter day. King Solomon's wedding procession (3:6 – 11), interposed about halfway through the love song, serves as a vivid picture of the strength, honor, and sheer beauty of marriage — of believers becoming one with the living God. The bride's dark night of the soul is followed by the longest and most poignant declaration of love by God the bridegroom in the entire Song of Songs, as if he is saying, "It's all right. Don't worry. I promise you, it's all right. I'm here."

> *How beautiful you are, my darling!*
>   *Oh, how beautiful!...*
> *Your lips are like a scarlet ribbon;*
>   *your mouth is lovely....*
> *All beautiful you are, my darling;*
>   *there is no flaw in you....*

You have stolen my heart, my sister, my bride;
        you have stolen my heart
with one glance of your eyes,
        with one jewel of your necklace.
How delightful is your love, my sister, my bride!
        How much more pleasing is your love than wine,
and the fragrance of your perfume than any spice!...
You are a garden locked up, my sister, my bride;
        you are a spring enclosed, a sealed fountain.
Your plants are an orchard of pomegranates
        with choice fruits,
        with henna and nard,
        nard and saffron,
        calamus and cinnamon,
        with every kind of incense tree,
        with myrrh and aloes
        and all the finest spices.

Song 4:1, 3, 7, 9–10, 12–14

In response to this the young bride invites her man to make love to her: "Awake, north wind, and come, south wind! Blow on my garden, that its fragrance may spread abroad. Let my lover come into his garden and taste its choice fruits" (4:16).

The bridegroom, the husband, responds and consummates their marriage: "I have come into my garden, my sister, my bride; I have gathered my myrrh with my spice. I have eaten my honeycomb and my honey; I have drunk my wine and my milk" (5:1).

After this, he concludes by speaking to members of the wedding party, encouraging friends to find the same joy in marriage as he has found: "Eat, friends, and drink; drink your fill of love" (5:1 TNIV). The love between God and his people, his church, shimmers with beauty and spiritual ecstasy and the most heartfelt companionship possible—so much so that those who experience it can't help but call others to such intimacy.

The Italian garden and the Japanese garden offer intimacy in different ways. The Japanese garden is simpler but no less profound. The flow of water (real or symbolized by intricately raked gravel), rocks, a stone lantern, a teahouse, stepping-stones or a bridge, a fence or hedge or wall to enclose the whole—all this reminds me of finding intimacy with God during those times of our lives when things are sparse and lean. There is still much beauty and harmony if we will but see it. My sister and her husband placed various parts of a Japanese garden in their backyard in the Pacific Northwest. Although the trees tower and the grass blazes green all year round, the smallness of a stone bridge, a pond, and a stone lantern is not lost amid the grandeur and offers its own statement on the spiritual nature of our lives.

My brother, on the other hand, built an Italian garden in his backyard, and this garden utilizes a quite different approach from that of my sister's: tall trees deliberately planted for effect, grassy slopes, hedges and statues and benches, a large fountain splashing in the center—it's like meditating at the edge of a forest. "There you may sit and enjoy clear, brilliant days," wrote Renaissance architect Leon Battista Alberti in the 1400s, "and beautiful prospects over wooded hills and sunlit plains, and listen to the murmuring fountains among the tufted grass."* This is a garden on a larger scale than the Japanese one, yet it offers an intimacy with God in a robust fashion that can also bless the spirit and bring important truths to light.

However, seasons change and gardens that once offered an opportunity for intimacy and reflection are lost to us due to biting winds, cold, and snow. In the same way, in the gardens of En Gedi, somehow the love of the bride, the church, cools. The church sleeps, though at the heart, there is still a vague awareness (Song 5:2). God knocks at the door and asks to be let in. His people are lethargic and irritable, as if his arrival were a nuisance: "I have taken off my robe — must I put it on again? I have washed my feet — must I soil them again?" (5:3). The love of God will not be put off. He slips his hand through the latch-opening in order to open the door (5:4). This finally awakens God's people. They rise and unlock the door. But God is gone: "I opened for my lover, but my lover had left; he was gone. My heart sank at his departure. I looked for him but did not find him. I called him but he did not answer" (5:6).

Again the bride runs in pursuit of her beloved, her husband, whom she has wronged. Perhaps she is not fully dressed. More than likely, her hair is not combed and is in disarray. This time, the night watchmen have nothing but contempt for her. She looks wild to them. Perhaps they see her as a menace, or a street person, or a half-naked prostitute. They beat her. They wound her. Soldiers from the walls come and strip the cloak off her

---

* Quoted in Christopher Thacker, *The History of Gardens* (Berkeley: University of California Press, 1985), 95.

back. We get an image of someone naked and bleeding and left facedown on the road in a swoon: "Daughters of Jerusalem, I charge you—if you find my lover, what will you tell him? Tell him I am faint with love" (5:8).

The allusions are too numerous to ignore. God comes to his people, but they are indifferent. They miss the opportunity to welcome him into their lives. And as a result, the bride, his own people who would not open the door to him, is stripped and wounded and must call out for rescue. And in the next garden, Gethsemane, the beloved will rescue his lover, and the beating and wounding he will take upon himself.

This traumatic night of separation, with the bride lovesick for the vanished bridegroom, is followed immediately by the bride's exclamation of love. She describes his beauty much as he described hers after her emergence from the first darkness:

> *My lover is radiant and ruddy,*
> *outstanding among ten thousand....*
> *His eyes are like doves*
> *by the water streams....*
> *His cheeks are like beds of spice....*
> *His appearance is like Lebanon,*
> *choice as its cedars.*
> *His mouth is sweetness itself;*
> *he is altogether lovely.*

Song 5:10, 12, 13, 15, 16

This passage culminates in one of the most wonderful expressions of intimacy in the whole love story: "I am my lover's, and my lover is mine" (6:3).

Once again, after the darkness, pain, and blood, her lover has returned to her. And the first thing the lover does is once again tell his bride how incredible she is: "You are as beautiful as Tirzah, my darling, as lovely as Jerusalem" (6:4 TNIV). He goes on to confess that he had visited a garden of nut trees to examine the new growth when he was surprised by his bride's renewed ardor for him: "I did not recognize myself; she made me a prince chosen from myriads of my people" (6:12 REB).

Estrangement between God and his people births a night of blood and nakedness. But the love of the church for her God and God for his church is only redoubled with the return of the sun. The church realizes once again how much God's love means to all of them, and God's passion for his people is as emotionally and spiritually charged as ever. The people's reinvigorated love for and worship of God have brought out his true colors of royalty. Whatever he was before, we see him now as he truly is — a prince. The romance is more powerful than ever.

There are more words of love as God watches his bride dance (6:13 – 7:9). She responds with a desire for love and intimacy, rising out of a renewed and stronger sense of her lover's undivided devotion for her: "I belong to my lover, and his desire is for me. Come, my lover, let us go to the countryside, let us spend the night in the villages" (7:10 – 11).

The love song concludes with further exclamations of desire and expressions of joy. The most forceful words of the song are found here, words that depict the heart of the poem. God says to his people, in the middle of all the love and happiness, "Place me like a seal over your heart, like a seal on your arm; for love is as strong as death" (8:6). The nights of turmoil in the song have proved that. The most beautiful mornings and the most radiant declarations of love have come after the cruelest experiences. In the end, God and his bride—his people, his church—are in the garden of love for good. But the garden is not so much a place in which God and his people meet and love one another; the garden is the people themselves. "Blow on my garden," they say, "that its fragrance may spread abroad. Let my lover come into his garden and taste its choice fruits" (4:16).

SEVEN

Some have suggested that the Song of Songs is an easier book for women to get into than men. On its most basic level, I don't think the Song of Songs is difficult for a man, at least, not for any man who has fallen in love and romanced a woman. A male reader simply takes on the role of the bridegroom and enjoys the poetry from the bridegroom's point of view. It is when the Song of Songs is viewed as a spiritual allegory, in addition to being a celebration of human love, that problems may arise.

For most women, viewing the Song of Songs from the bride's angle is comfortable, and when the poetry is taken as an allegorical expression of love between God and his bride, the transition from physical bride to spiritual bride is a natural one. Not so for most men. They feel they must somehow make a switch from being a physical bridegroom to a spiritual bride—and the changeover is not comfortable. It is hard to take in the intense romantic symbolism coming at them from God, where God is the male figure and suddenly they are female figures.

I believe the Song of Songs is approachable for men if they come at it in the right way. First of all, they can certainly identify with the male protagonist at the allegorical level as well as the physical. They should find it easy to get into God's skin. They know what it is like to be in love, to get caught up with someone, to plan dates, send flowers, select restaurants with the right ambience. These experiences can be obsessive, exhilarating, and discouraging all at once. Therefore, a man is in an excellent position to understand what it means when the Bible, here or anywhere, states that God loves his people.

In some ways, as they take on the male role of bridegroom, men know what it is like to be God. They see the fire of his love, and they've known that kind of fire for a woman. Obstacles get in the way, and God sweeps them aside. Thorns rise up in the path, and God slashes through them with his sword. Men know all about being princes racing to the rescue on white chargers and fighting for those they love. Indeed, this kind of roaring love a man may experience not only for his own bride but for his own children too. Reading the Song of Songs, seeing spiritual love from God's viewpoint, seeing its intensity, a man is on comfortable ground because he knows that intensity. A man would die for his son, for his daughter, for his bride. So he understands how God would die for his children, his people, his bride. All of a sudden, the allegorical is not so difficult to swallow. Men see where God is coming from, because it is where many of them are coming from. They appreciate that this is how God feels not only about them as men, but how he feels about their families and friends — and they feel moved by God's mutual concern and commitment.

Secondly, many men have known what it is to be truly loved, and once they have experienced it, they will never forget it. When they have known, for instance, a woman's love and friendship, support and strength, it is something they want more of, not less. When they have known the love and devotion of their children, it puts them on top of the world. The love and friendship of brothers and sisters is not experienced by every man, but when it is, it is something solid and strong; it is holy ground. And when a man has friends outside the family — men and women who value him, accept him as he is, and enjoy being around him — it is the icing on the cake. Toss in the love of an animal companion, and it doesn't get any better.

Approaching it from this point of view, a man should not have a hard time hearing that God loves and likes him. It is love, and he understands love. It's just that God's love is on a much larger scale; it is more radical, more powerful, more transforming, more awesome than anything he has ever experienced. At the same time, though, it is just as real, just as significant, just as down to earth, just as manly, as any other good love he is grateful for.

All of the intensity of God's love, from whatever angle, may be felt by any woman as well. But for women who have been hurt by men or hurt in marriage, it is, of course, not as easy to read the Song of Songs. They may have seen this kind of romantic intensity before and watched it turn to ashes before their eyes. They may have had some of this same poetry recited to them in a marriage vow or in a relationship. They may have been beaten by a man who quoted from the Song of Songs. This is the same anguish experienced by women who have been sexually abused by their fathers and no longer have the freedom within to call God a father. This is true for men too. Experiences of bad marriages and romances that went sour can make a reading of the Song a painful experience.

There is another difficulty men and women share, namely, spiritual abuse. Pastors and church leaders have told them all about the love of God, Sunday after Sunday, yet scarcely a drop of that love got through to them from the people in the churches themselves, people who seemed to take every opportunity to hang them out to dry. What does God's love mean after someone has experienced these kinds of things? Then add a perception that God himself has personally abused them — not answering their prayers, standing by while their daughter died in a house fire, permitting their mother to commit suicide or their son to suffer from depression and wind up in a psychiatric ward. "God doesn't keep the promises found in the Bible. He is anything but kind and loving. He can't be trusted," they conclude.

Some of these people may run to God for a love they have never known and find it, despite broken marriages, anger at God, or a prolonged dark night of the soul in which nothing has made spiritual sense for years; others become jaded and sit in En Gedi unmoved, like the stone statues of the Italian garden — present but hardened to the beauty and wonder of God's love. They have known spiritual and physical suffering on such a scale they have lost all faith in humanity and in God, and no words, however well put, can move them. They hear us tell them that all around them is the garden of love. They hear someone say, "The garden of love is within you if you believe it." But it means nothing to them.

The watchmen came upon them one night, wherever they were, and wounded them and tore the clothes of belief off their back. They have made up their minds — or have had their minds made up for them—that they can never be healed. They may sit in En Gedi for a long time before they ask about the night passages of the Song, before they ask about the myrrh and the beating and the blood, before they ask about the alienation and the abandonment. Then they may need to go to the third garden, Gethsemane, and see the horror of a dying God before their eyes focus a little differently. In time, they may make their way back to En Gedi, where its poetry and beauty can fan a flame within them.

But for those who are able to be in the garden of love and see it for what it is, the experience can be life changing—as true love always is. This garden is about the truest and longest love. It is about a God who will not stop romancing us, about his love for us in the cold and mist of the darkness and right through the heat of the day. The person who takes just a bit of this into his or her soul will find good reason to relish life.

If you hear God say these strong words—"Place me like a seal over your heart, like a seal on your arm, for love is as strong as death"—and realize they are directed at you personally, this will be enough to shift the planets of your life and create a new personal universe. From the beginning of time, human beings have hoped that death is not the greatest god and that its word is not the final word. If you and I understand En Gedi, then we will know the truth: love is the final word, and *nothing* can separate us from God's love. Not only will we have come to the garden and breathed in this beauty and truth; we will realize *we* are the very ones whom God loves.

PART THREE

GETHSEMANE
The GARDEN *of* DEATH

When he had finished praying, Jesus left with
his disciples and crossed the Kidron Valley.
On the other side there was a garden,
and he and his disciples went into it.
John 18:1 TNIV

ONE

A visit with Jessie and Isaac wasn't your normal pastoral call. There was no sitting down to a cup of tea, no photo albums of the grandkids. Jessie and Isaac were active and energetic, and they didn't sit down long anywhere. They curled and fished and hunted and traveled. And when they were at their home, they were just as much outside their house as inside it. The backyard was one small part grass and one large part garden. They were always in that garden together, harvesting, weeding, planting. And putting up more and more fencing, for the deer were fleet of foot and leaped over virtually any barrier to munch on what Jessie and Isaac had grown. Black bears shouldered their massive bulks into the garden plot too, I had seen them often enough, slipping like great shadows through the tall trees in the neighborhood, eyes darting toward neat rows of lettuce and cabbage and beets. In a way this garden was a full-time job, but Jessie and Isaac liked it that way.

On one visit, I walked around the house to find Jessie in the garden, but Isaac was nowhere to be seen. An ax was leaning against a chopping block, ready to use, and all kinds of logs were stacked up to be split, but Isaac wasn't there.

Jessie pushed back stray strands of blonde hair from her flushed face and smiled, gloved hands holding a pair of gardening shears. "He had to get some wedges to drive into the bigger logs so he could break them apart easier. Won't be long. Unless he finds someone to talk to about fishing or hunting. Would you like some iced tea?"

I didn't actually. And frankly, I didn't want to just sit around either. Isaac cheered for the wrong football team, and I felt a keen sense of competition surging up in me. "I'll show him how wood can be split without wedges," I told her with a cocky smile on my face as I picked up the ax.

It was a bit of a contest between me and the guy who cheered for the wrong team. Truth be told, I wasn't a novice to chopping logs. Besides, I wanted the workout. So I flew at the stack and really did let the chips fall where they may. Log after log was split and tossed aside. The longer you chop, the easier you swing and the faster you cut. Isaac's stack shrunk quickly.

When I stopped, about a half hour had gone by. I planted the axhead firmly in the chopping block and looked around. Jessie was grinning. Log halves and quarters were strewn everywhere, white and fresh and open to the sun like dozens of cut apples. I began piling the split wood, but then I shook my head.

"On second thought, Jessie," I said, "if I pick it up, he'll forget and think he did it. If I leave it this way, he'll know it was someone else. I think I'll leave this part for him."

"Sure," she said with a laugh.

So I left for home, chopped wood strewn all about.

That fall, Jessie and Isaac brought baskets and baskets of produce from their garden to place at the altar at the front of the church. Several other families joined in, and in the end the church generously insisted my wife and I take the harvest home. Isaac never mentioned the wood-chopping incident, and the wrong team lost to the right team that autumn, so the only thing I got from him was a sharp gleam of defiance in his eyes. But Jessie pulled me aside one morning and smiled, "Not too much impresses Isaac, but I want you to know he was impressed that day he came back from his errand. It saved him a lot of time. He got to spend a few extra hours in the garden — which he loves."

This all took place on Vancouver Island, just off the coast of British Columbia and northwest of Washington State. After a few years, Jessie and Isaac moved back to their home province of Alberta so they could be closer to their grandchildren and family. This time they didn't have a backyard; they had an acreage, really a small farm, and they could have grown vegetables for miles if they'd wanted to. The grandkids came over often, and there were quads to ride, deer to hunt, trout to catch, gardens to seed in May and harvest each summer and fall — the kind of paradise Jessie and Isaac had been dreaming of. The kind of place you settle right into, where you can live out the rest of your days in wonder and peace with family all around.

Early one December morning, just before Christmas, Jessie and Isaac got up in their typically good mood and went to collect wood just a few miles from their place. They got a load and headed back, the sun not quite up, and as Isaac made a turn from the woods onto a main road, a semitrailer slammed into them at full speed. Someone called 911, and after being freed from the wreckage, they were both airlifted to the hospital. On the way, emergency personnel fought to keep them alive. Isaac drifted in and out of consciousness. Then he was gone. And they could not get him back.

Amazingly, Jessie survived. She battled through many hard, painful days and weeks, but she made it. My wife and I gently took her in our arms the morning of Isaac's funeral — her body was still so fragile — and we cried with her, as family and friends gathered all around us in a small house of wooden walls and bright Christmas decorations. Though I had been asked to officiate at many funerals by that point in my ministry, I found the graveside experience hard — the flowers of summer in the sharp winter air, the turned earth, the dark hole and the coffin. We put Isaac's body in the ground just as we would plant a cluster of tulip bulbs. Tulip bulbs are planted in the hope that after months of snow and frost, flowers of every imaginable color will emerge in the soft-edged air of spring. But there would be no such miracle of new life for Isaac; knowing this made the December cold bite more sharply and the winter frost penetrate more deeply right down into our souls.

TWO

The warm waters and bright sun of En Gedi yield to the coolness and shadows of Gethsemane. It is the garden of night. Yet it is no less a garden of love than En Gedi. It is only that En Gedi's love was out in the open and obvious; Gethsemane's is wrapped in darkness and hidden.

As humans, we are not unfamiliar with gardens like this. Places of sheer agony, of broken dreams, broken hearts, and broken lives. We have been in the shadows often enough and cried out desperately to God more than once. We understand this garden better than all the others. We have worn ruts in its grass with our pacing. A person smells blood in this garden. And cruelty. A person touches hell in this garden. If it is true that love is here but hidden, it is also true that for many of us that hiding place has never been found. We may know the garden of suffering well, but we do not know it as well as we should like. Of all places in which we most need to experience the love of God, this is the place we experience it least. Every blade of grass in it we recognize, every stiff flower, every sharp bush. But what we most need to recognize we cannot see.

Yet it is humanity that has made this garden. Of all the biblical gardens, Gethsemane and the Garden Tomb are the ones most fashioned by human fingers and shovels. We planted

Gethsemane's olive trees. And if some were already there, it is still true that we have tended them all. We have planted the flowers, pulled up the weeds, tilled the soil. We still do. Go, take your camera; you can photograph this garden. You cannot photograph the beginning or the end—you cannot take pictures of the first Eden or the final Eden. But En Gedi, Gethsemane, the Garden Tomb, these you can see for yourself and take images home and frame them. The journey between Eden and Eden we can hold in our hands; we can touch it, taste it, fill our nostrils with it. It is still our journey. We still walk it, and this is why it is still with us. We have left, but we have not arrived.

Jesus went to the garden to pray. He opened the gate made by human hands with his own human hand. He entered a garden humans had created. Here, where the curses of Eden would begin to be unwound, humanity had erected the fence. A crude imitation it may be, but this garden fence still represents the encircling arms of God's love. Jesus chose to come inside that fence.

Throughout his life, Jesus prayed in wild places and lonely places. Consider Mark 6:46, where Peter, whose memoir the gospel of Mark is, recalls that "after leaving [the crowd], [Jesus] went up on a mountainside to pray." Or look at Luke 5:16: "Jesus often withdrew to lonely places and prayed." Or what about another night, something of a parallel to the Gethsemane night, when Jesus had a different choice to make and prayed on the mountainside until sunrise before choosing the twelve disciples (Luke 6:12)? Yet on this night, the night before his death, Jesus does not go on a mountainside or into the wilderness; he goes inside a garden.

He could have left the city to pray; he could have gone out among the owls and jackals. But spending time on the Mount of Olives was something of a habit when Jesus was in Jerusalem, as Luke suggests in 22:39 (and John in his gospel at 18:2). So this night he again unlatched the gate, went in, and started to pray. Pray as he had never prayed in his life. One could offer by way of explanation: "He wanted Judas to find him." That may be true. But it does not lessen the impact of what is taking place: What we lost in a garden will be found in a garden. What we lost in a God-created garden will be found in a human-created garden. In Eden, God placed humans in his own garden; in Gethsemane, the Son of God is placed in our own garden. What was planted in the midst of the human predicament will be the site where the unraveling of that human predicament begins.

The mix of the human with the divine in the redemption of the human race is not confined to Gethsemane. We make the nails that kill Jesus, but God made the iron ore from which the nails were forged. We made the cross; God made the wood. We made the whip that scourged Jesus; God made the animals whose skins provided the leather for the whip. Jesus carried the cross, but we carried it too—and our name was Simon. The body of Jesus was placed in a tomb carved out of the rock by human hands, but God made the rock. Redemption, in more ways than one, has a human face.

Jesus enters the garden that we humans know intimately, the garden of pain and death. It is Passover, and Passover is always aligned with a full moon. If there are no clouds, the olive trees are silver in the white light. In Eden, there was a choice; in

Gethsemane, there is a choice. Jesus separates himself from the eleven disciples. What will happen now separates this garden from all other gardens.

Gethsemane is at the center of the biblical gardens — two before, two after. If there is going to be a second Eden, if God is going to dwell with humanity, if human exile is going to end, then it is going to happen here or not at all. Jesus makes the choice to be or not to be the Passover lamb in this garden on this night. Much happens after the full moon is down. Much happens after Jesus goes back out through the gate. But all of it is a direct consequence of what happens in the garden itself. Either the angel of death will pass over and spare the human race, or it will not. But if it passes over the human race, it will not pass over the God with a human face. There will be blood shed because of what Jesus prays in this garden on this night.

You will never see the Son of God more human than in this garden. "He began to be sorrowful and troubled," recalls Matthew (26:37). "My soul," Jesus said, "is overwhelmed with sorrow to the point of death" (26:38). Sharing the same story, Mark affirms, "He began to be deeply distressed and troubled" (Mark 14:33). "Pray that you will not fall into temptation," Jesus tells his disciples (Luke 22:40). But he himself will be spared none of it. Like the Christmas story, Easter can either gain power in repeated tellings or lose power. If we cannot see the pain of Jesus here, then we have lost something important. And in doing so, we will lose some of the ability to measure the value of our own grief.

The ugliness of the night has fastened its reeking claws into

Jesus. Confusion has frozen a piece of his mind. The anticipation of extreme and enduring pain, every nerve end shriek-
ing and screeching, has disemboweled him. The human race
is not there for him — "Couldn't you men keep watch with me
for one hour?" (Matthew 26:40 TNIV) — and soon, neither is
God: *"Eli, Eli, lema sabachthani?"* (27:46 TNIV) — My God,
my God, my Father, why have you also despised me and averted
your eyes?

If, as Frederick Buechner points out, God in diapers is a
scandal,* what about the scandal of the cross, what about the
scandal of a God bleeding? Which is more difficult to take
in — God soiling himself as a crying infant at birth, or God soiling himself as a crying man at death? We put both Christmas and
Easter sentiments on pretty cards, but both events are absurdities
that moved heaven and earth. And it is between heaven and earth
that Jesus hangs at Golgotha, scorned by humanity and divinity.

Humans see a fool, a risk, and a fraud; a few see a dead hero.
God sees Auschwitz and Dachau, Hiroshima and Nagasaki,
Rwanda and Sudan, gassed Kurds and slaughtered Armenians,
flies crawling out of a slain baby's nostrils. The Crusades, the
sack of Constantinople, the storming of Jerusalem. The dead
from car blasts, body parts from the work of attack helicopters
and suicide bombers. Warfare and terrorism and genocide hang
in the sky, rape and child murder and serial killing, lies and
deceit and vengeance. Hell. A bloody head is on a pole at The
Place of the Skull. Are there any of us who could take that evil

---

* Frederick Buechner, *The Faces of Jesus* (Brewster, Mass.: Paraclete, 2005), 20 – 21.

on our backs? Let it crush the breath and heart out of us? He saves the sex-trade worker and the Palestinian and the Israeli; he saves the boy with dark eyes in the Russian classroom from the guns and bombs of Chechen rebels, but himself he cannot save.

Unless he does not drink. If he puts the cup down full, he will live. And we will die. Why not? Are we so very special? Is the human race worth this? Do we equal the life of a God? Are we a proper exchange for all light, all good, all that is true, all that is love? "My Father, if it is possible, may this cup be taken from me" (Matthew 26:39). History and literature are full of cups such as this. "Gertrude, do not drink!" cries the king to his queen in Hamlet. She drinks and dies. "Do not drink the hemlock!" cry Socrates' disciples. He drinks and dies. "Father, if you are willing, take this cup from me," cries Jesus (Luke 22:42). But the cup is not taken from him. He is nailed hand and foot to a cross. And dies.

THREE

My brother is the painter in the family; I am the writer. But sometimes I think I would like to take a dozen canvases, an easel, a palette, and a brush and spread color over the blankness and the white and create images as he does. Once I thought of making a series of paintings on the crucifixion—but not as you'd normally think such a series would look.

The first would be of a man in a business suit, half kneeling, half sprawled by the side of a bed in a house. His suit is rumpled, his tie unknotted. He is middle-aged, about fifty years old, round-faced, losing his hair. He looks completely exhausted, bewildered, and defeated. Behind him the horizontal blinds are open, and light is coming in and putting stripes of brightness and shadow on the side of his face—in fact, over the whole room. On the bed is a person who has just died—and this image is striped bright and dark as well. It is a daughter or a son or maybe this man's wife. One of his hands grasps the person's hand, but that hand is limp. This man is totally destroyed by what has just occurred. The title of the painting? *Unanswered Prayer*.

The next painting would be Jesus on the cross. I would try not to make it look too dramatic or romantic. Christians are masters at romanticizing the Bible stories, making them suitable for children under ten, and by so doing tearing the honest-to-

God guts and reality out of them. The sweet birth in a perfect stable. The sweet flight into Egypt. The sweet dance of Salome that results in the beheading of John the Baptist. The dramatic death of Christ. The dramatic stoning of Stephen. The dramatic arrival of the antichrist on earth. How exciting! No, Jesus is tortured to death and bled white—it is not romantic, and it is not enthralling. It's as ugly and as dirty as death gets. This won't be a pretty painting. The title? *Unanswered Prayer*.

The final painting in the series I'm not sure about. Maybe a family having a picnic in a summer campground—lots of light, lots of green leaves and grass, lots of laughter. Or maybe a man fly-fishing in a rugged canyon—fast water pouring silver as he wades into the high mountain river, shadows and splashes of gold, his face set in determination, anticipation, and the joy of being one with water, rock, and air. Or maybe a woman sitting alone at a table with a cup of coffee, peace on her face, in her hands, in her eyes, even though all around her you see wreaths and notes of sympathy and all the memorial flowers of death. A child is gone, a husband, too soon, but she has an unnatural strength. This painting, as you may have guessed, is also called *Unanswered Prayer*. All these images of a family, a fly fisherman, a woman link back to the unanswered prayer of the cross. The startling reality is that because Jesus' prayer was not answered, many of ours are, and thus it is a different world.

FOUR

The choice to accept the unanswered prayer is not easily made. For man and woman, taking the fruit in Eden was easy compared to this man accepting the cup in Gethsemane. They did not see the consequences; he does. Sweat like drops of blood. "*Abba*," Jesus cries out, "*Abba*, Daddy, help me, please. I do not want to become the selfishness and the lies and the cruelty of the human race. The thought of becoming evil, all evil, torments me to the bone. No, my Father, no." In the apostle Paul's words, "God made him who had no sin to be sin for us, so that in him we might become the righteousness of God" (2 Corinthians 5:21).

Somewhere in the soil of Gethsemane today, I might imagine that the salt of Jesus' sweat is still present in one form or another. If angels leave footprints, I might imagine I see an imprint on a rock. Without knowing it, I might stand where James and John watched and slept. I might walk the path that Judas walked.

Humanity slept at Gethsemane. Humanity broke through the gate with torches and clubs. Humanity was Judas. Humanity was the law and the temple police. Humanity was the violence. Humanity was the lynching of God.

"Who is it you want?"
"Jesus of Nazareth."

"I am." (The soldiers and police step back and fall to the ground.)

"Who is it you want?"

"Jesus of Nazareth."

"I told you. I am."

John 18:4 – 8, my translation

Jesus speaks the name that God spoke to Moses out of the burning bush, the divine name, I AM, YHWH (Exodus 3:14). It is no coincidence of Greek syntax or grammar. The very power of the name is like a blow that forces the mob back, prostrate. The garden is holy ground.

A sword flash as Peter slices off a man's ear. Human blood on the holy ground. But in this night garden a healing of that blood. "Put your sword away!" Jesus tells Peter. "Shall I not drink the cup the Father has given me?" (John 18:11). And he adds, not just to Peter, "All who use swords are destroyed by swords" (Matthew 26:52 MSG). There was a sword at Eden; now there are swords again on this night when the gateway to the second Eden is being opened. But there is no holiness to these swords of darkness. These are the sort of weapons that will be beaten into plowshares at the advent of that final Eden.

And the promise of the new Eden, the new garden, is confirmed by the restoration of the wounded man's ear. The healing makes no difference to the mob. Jesus is seized. The disciples run. The One who is both the Son of God and the Son of Man is forced from the garden. There is still a dampness on his cheek, almost dry, from the kiss. A far cry from the passionate kisses and the intense devotion of En Gedi. In this garden, the kisses of humanity are not faithful devotion but betrayal.

The rest of the story will play itself out in the city and on the hill—spit, scourging, thorns, a pocketful of nails in an Italian hand. But the decision was made behind the fence, behind the enclosure, in a place of solitude and struggle and prayer. Without Gethsemane there is no Golgotha, no *Calvaria* (the Latin word for "skull").

It had taken some time to make that choice. Perhaps several hours. When Jesus' birth was announced, there were angels. When he makes his choice to accept the cup of sacrifice, there is an angel again—to give him the strength to go through with it. He was Adam as much as he was God. The temptation was real: to choose to die for the sins of the world or not. Still, in the middle of the struggle, it was always, "Yet not my will, but yours be done" (Luke 22:42). In the blaze of moonlight, every tree illuminated, every leaf etched, every fern and flower glistening, he obeyed the light and, in so doing, walked into the darkness.

For all his struggle in the garden there is none of it remaining once he has been hustled out the gate. Resolute, he faces taunts and jeers and whips and nails. Immovable, he stands before earthly powers—religion in the form of the Sanhedrin, empire in the form of Pilate and Rome, monarchy in the form of Herod, majority rule in the form of the mob that shouts for his death. He is unflinching. He has made his choice.

The decision in Gethsemane will undo the decision in Eden. In Eden, those who represented humanity failed the test; in Gethsemane, the one who represented humanity did not. In

Eden, the innocent were corrupted; in Gethsemane, the innocent died for the corrupted. Gethsemane not only stands at the center of the biblical gardens; indeed, it is at the center of human history and the center of our universe. It creates a new humanity and a new world. All that was meant to be can now be. There is no garden like Gethsemane, the garden in the dark that unwinds the dark. It is the epicenter of the earthquake of God's love.

FIVE

I had a younger brother who was born with cerebral palsy. My mother's umbilical cord cut off his oxygen. There should have been a C-section; there wasn't, and after his birth he was mentally challenged, his body was torn by seizures, and he struggled to live all of his short life. But he was beautiful. I loved to play with him and make him laugh. I prayed and prayed for him to be healed. I envisioned the whole family coming to faith in Christ because of his healing, all of us Christians together, worshiping together—it was wonderful. But when my brother was twenty, he had a final seizure, went into a coma, and died. I was far away in Israel when it happened. A lifetime of prayers had changed nothing. Death had brought darkness to me.

And more darkness came out of that darkness. My mother never did recover from her guilt over the state in which my brother was born. She experienced severe depression, was heavily medicated, and eventually became institutionalized, leaving my father to care for my older brother and sister and me. Dad's own depression often boiled over into rage. It was a bewildering and painful time for me. I was eleven or twelve, and it crushed my heart.

Mom eventually returned home, but she was never the same after her years in the asylum. She actually became a Christian in the midst of that darkness, and I saw how the Bible and prayer and the hymns she played on the organ in our house brought her a measure of peace. Yet the shadows still flitted about her eyes. Ten years after my brother died, she took her own life.

I recall the morning after the phone call. The sunset was bloodred, vivid as a gash. Whatever pain I had felt before in my brief lifetime was nothing compared to what I was feeling now. My insides felt as though they were being carved up. I looked to God, I prayed, I agonized—no part of the story of my brother and my mother had worked out as I had hoped to God it would. The sunrise was like night to me.

In the garden, Jesus was in the dark, and he was afraid of the dark. This creates an instant bond with each of us. We, too, have been in the dark and been afraid there. We have been in the dark and suffered there. If Jesus has been there, then we have someone who comprehends what others sometimes can't—the heaviness in such black holes, the anxiety, the anger, the weakness, the claustrophobia, the inability to focus, the inability to believe, the aloneness, the lostness, the hopelessness, the loss of margins and boundaries and purpose. "Because he himself suffered when he was tempted," the writer of Hebrews declares, "he is able to help those who are being tempted" (2:18).

The love hidden in the shadows of Gethsemane is not that the day will come when we will cease to suffer between the first Eden and the Second Eden; it is that God suffers what we suffer and by doing so redeems not only our suffering but, much more, redeems us. He never trivializes what breaks our hearts. It put nails into him. There is no pain we wrestle with that he will scoff at. All the sin, suffering, and temptation we experience, all the misery that breaks us—it broke him too. The pain we deal with as victims—that pain Jesus took with him to the cross and bled it out. It is not just Darfur or 9/11 or the drug wars in Colombia he takes to the hilltop; it is you and me and our whole little worlds. No person, no life, no tragedy, no guilt was forgotten.

It is enough if you come to Gethsemane in your mind and spirit and realize the extent of the sacrifice Jesus is about to make. If you can imagine Jesus there, his anguish practically killing him, finally deciding to go ahead and die so that you are free to return to Paradise and to God—if you can grasp even a small part of this—you will have grasped what many scarcely brush with their thoughts in a lifetime.

When Jesus made his choice to move ahead in obedience to the will of God the Father, he crushed the adversary's head while taking the wound on his own heel. He took the bite of spikes and spear and whip. He made possible the restoration of Eden, an existence devoid of grief and sin and destruction, but brimming with joy and goodness and unending, untarnished life. It is a monumental truth to take in, and many never get their minds around it. They spend their years trying to do things to get God to like them when, in fact, God already loves them and sent his Son to heal the break between humanity and divinity. Eugene Peterson puts it elegantly and concisely:

> Since the children are made of flesh and blood, it's logical that the Savior took on flesh and blood in order

to rescue them by his death. By embracing death, taking it into himself, he destroyed the Devil's hold on death and freed all who cower through life, scared to death of death.

It's obvious, of course, that he didn't go to all this trouble for angels. It was for people like us, children of Abraham. That's why he had to enter into every detail of human life. Then, when he came before God as high priest to get rid of the people's sins, he would have already experienced it all himself—all the pain, all the testing—and would be able to help where help was needed.

Hebrews 2:14–18 MSG

Bit by bit, as you roam around in the garden of the heart, spending time in Eden, spending time in En Gedi, it dawns on you that although there are many biblical gardens, there is only one in which someone is praying. And in Gethsemane, the garden of prayer, the prayer that is being prayed is to know and do the will of God—and the answer to the prayer is crucifixion. This can come as something of a shock. To tell the truth, we do not expect Gethsemane to be a comfortable garden seat. It is, after all, the place in which Jesus was betrayed and arrested and hauled off to an ugly end. But it may jar us to realize that for Jesus to know and do the will of God meant his death.

The Christianity of North America is a luxurious Christianity. For the most part, there are plenty of cars and televisions and DVD players, plenty of vacations to exotic destinations. The houses are big, the churches are big, and there is a lot of money to go around. It is not the same for Christians in much of the rest of the world — places where there is poverty and persecution. In North America, Christians are taken aback to think the will of God could involve their own death. In other parts of the world, Christians see death as a distinct possibility — why shouldn't they die for their faith? Jesus died. The apostles died. Throughout the centuries Christians have died. It has been the will of God for many.

In a culture in which the highest goals are pleasure and ease and longevity, taking this reality in is like swallowing nails. It is one thing to sit in the garden and gradually come to comprehend that God's love for you is so intense that Jesus was crucified for you; it is something else again to think about you yourself being crucified like Christ. Could God really ask you to give your life? Would he?

Jesus cried out for help in the garden, and we understand that. He wrestled with God, asking that he be spared the agony and the suffering, and we understand that too. The fact that his prayer was not answered, or at least not answered in the way he asked, well, we know how that feels by bitter experience. Tempted to do what is less than the best, that is a battle we also know. Fear of the dark, fear of pain, fear of abandonment — we are one with Jesus in all of it.

What begins to happen in Gethsemane, without our noticing it at first, is that we merge with Jesus. His fears are our fears, his struggles our struggles, and then we see that our fears are his, our struggles are his. Increasingly, we give all our wars and our weeping to him. He takes them, redeems them, and gives them back, but they feel different, because they are. We feel different, because we are. We begin to look at our sufferings the way he looks at them, to talk about them the way he talks about them, to experience them the way he experiences them. Passages in Scripture we did not understand before begin to make sense: "I gave up all that inferior stuff so I could know Christ personally, experience his resurrection power, be a partner in his suffering, and go all the way with him to death itself," says Paul in Philippians 3:10 (MSG). But in his earlier letter to the Galatians, Paul gets even more to the point: "I have been crucified with Christ and I no longer live, but Christ lives in me. The life I live in the body, I live by faith in the Son of God, who loved me and gave himself for me" (Galatians 2:20). Eugene Peterson, in *The Message*, puts it this way:

> I identified myself completely with [Christ]. Indeed, I have been crucified with Christ. My ego is no longer central. It is no longer important that I appear righteous before you or have your good opinion, and I am no longer driven to impress God. Christ lives in me. The life you see me living is not "mine," but it is lived by faith in the Son of God, who loved me and gave himself for me. I am not going to go back on that.

SIX

No matter how ordinary we may feel we are, the longer we spend with Christ, the more we become like Christ. This is not so surprising. We are who our friends are. We take on the qualities of those we are closest to and those we most admire. There is a different twist with Jesus, however. If we become like him in life, we become like him in death. There can be no separation. The things that enliven him enliven us; the things that kill him kill us. Whatever he died to and died for we die to and die for. In our spirit and in our body. Whether our flesh and blood is slain becomes inconsequential in this sense. We are already dead. It is Jesus who makes us who we are, and Jesus is forever. Our bodies may fall to the ground like a pear from a tree. But our spirits are forever because they are one with the spirit of Jesus. "I no longer live, but Christ lives in me."

Do we lose our individuality? Our personality? What makes us unique? Think for a moment about some of the most spiritual people you know or admire—even if you just know them from a book, a television broadcast, or a conference you attended. Do all these men and women or even children look the same? Act the same? Have the same speaking or writing style? The same sense of humor? They are all different yet they are all caught up in Jesus Christ. What about the apostles and other followers of

Christ? Is Matthew's gospel a carbon copy of John's? Are Mark and Luke indistinguishable in terms of content and vocabulary? Are Peter's letters exactly like Paul's, or John's letters exactly like James's letter? Are Martin Luther and Martin Luther King Jr. identical twins? Are Mother Teresa and Teresa of Avila mirror images? Do all Christians act like Francis of Assisi? Are all capable of writing *The Imitation of Christ* or founding World Vision? Yet Christ simmers in all of them just the same, and it is in his spirit that they live and move and have their being. Merging with Christ only means you emerge as the human soul God always intended.

An odd place, this Garden of Gethsemane. It's all about death, and yet it bristles with life, particularly life never seen before on earth. It makes you and me something more unique than we were, and it does the same to the entire spinning earth. The shadows of Gethsemane hide more than we can guess.

But someone will come along and say, "This is all very interesting, but I want suffering to end now. I don't just want to be able to absorb it like Jesus absorbed it; I want it gone. I want it over with. I thought Jesus' choice in Gethsemane made the Second Eden a reality."

So it does. It starts in Gethsemane, spreads to the Garden Tomb, and brings the Second Eden to earth. But we have not yet arrived. We are caught in time; God is not. His spirit is in ours so we can sense the Second Eden and glimpse it from afar with spirit eyes, but our bodies are clay, and they cling to the clay of the gardens of the earth. In the garden of the heart, we can go to the second Eden and look around us and try to imagine what it is we are seeing; in the body we cannot. I can sit in Gethsemane and pray and think. I might be all the better for doing it. But the second Eden will still be on the inside. I will not be able to touch it. I will not be able to see it with the eyes of my flesh-and-blood body, except perhaps in glimpses in which I see a dog curling up with a kitten or a Palestinian embracing an Israeli or a body riddled with terminal cancer miraculously healed. When I am finally outside of time and there is only God's timelessness, when my body is made new like my soul and the whole earth is spring, when the wild geese return and the Holy Spirit rises with healing in his wings, that will be time enough to pause and smell the red roses of a new Eden and settle into the final garden for an eternity. Until then, I have "Christ in [me], the hope of glory" (Colossians 1:27). He is the garden at the end of the world. He is also the garden of God for all races and all centuries.

SEVEN

When my son turned one, he learned to walk and couldn't wipe the smile off his face. This was on Vancouver Island, where we had a large garden and all sorts of berry bushes. The two of us began to take strolls around the garden in the evening before he went to bed. This always involved a lot of berries winding up in his mouth. Yet even after the garden died that fall and the bushes failed to yield fruit, he still wanted to walk around and examine everything. So when it came time to burn the dead plants and stalks of the summer garden, we made a big deal of it.

"Look," I said to him, pointing as the match ignited the pile of debris. "Look, the garden is the color of fire." We fed the mound with a few more branches and dead vines. Red, yellow, blue, white, green, and orange sprang up in the darkness. It illuminated his face and mine. For a long time it gave us warmth. Then the flames dropped and vanished. We went to bed full of good cheer. We had, after all, created light.

The next morning, I raked the ashes into the garden. Now the bit of earth that had been large and vivid with growing things didn't look like much. No green. No fire. Dead and gone. But in a garden there really is no such thing. Something is always going on. It doesn't matter if cold rain seals the land, as it did for the garden of the bonfire, or deep snow, as with the garden of my boyhood. Death and decay are illusions. Good things come out of the ashes and the cold ground, good things that never existed before. There is no such thing as a dead garden, not in the whole wide world. When you think you see one, remember that there is more to it than meets the eye. A dead garden is a trick.

THE GARDEN TOMB

The GARDEN of IMMORTALITY

At the place where Jesus was crucified,
there was a garden, and in the garden a new
tomb, in which no one had ever been laid.
John 19:41

ONE

When we first looked at the house we now live in, I immediately noticed there had once been a fairly large garden in the backyard. It was a cold, blustery April day, and not much seemed to be trying to emerge from the soil except the raspberry canes—and they only looked half alive. In June, when we moved in, not much had changed. The raspberry canes had sprouted a few green leaves, a small plant or two had broken through the soil, and there were a lot of dandelions. The garden was pretty much dead. "The creek burst its banks back in '95," I was told by a neighbor. "The flood ruined a lot of things. Covered your backyard in clay and muck. Tore down a hundred-foot-long fence along the creek bed. This is new grass, you know. Rolls of sod. I helped lay it. But no one had time to do anything for the garden."

So I began to dig. Break up the clods. Add topsoil. Plant perennials. There was a lot of rain that summer, which is unusual for southwestern Alberta. Thunderstorm after thunderstorm roared over the mountains and onto the foothills and prairie. When it wasn't raining, it was hot. Broccoli thrived. Tomatoes ripened on the vine, dozens of them. Raspberries clustered like grapes. Nearby, an apple tree sagged with fruit. Each year, we tried to make improvements to the garden that had previously been left for dead. I was fascinated by the concept of perennials. Carnations went in. Columbine. Echinacea.

Most of it did well. Until I came to the northern end of the garden, the part closest to the creek that winds through our property. In this area of the garden, plants died and never grew back. Or they came up grudgingly and stopped cold after two or three inches. We tried everything we could think of. We bought fertilizer, used compost, added more topsoil, even planted the hardiest herbs in an attempt to get something to grow there.

It was a battle. Most of our summers are dry here. The first July and August of plenteous rainfall had been an anomaly. All the other years, sprinklers lashed the earth and hoses curled through the grass to help us hold a bit of ground against the heat of the bone-white sun. But the mint didn't make it, or the lemon balm. Sage and bergamot barely survived.

I thought if I added some decor to the garden, the plants might take heart and try harder. One spring, I lugged in large pieces of driftwood, rolled boulders into the corners, put up wrought-iron fencing. We planted and watered and fertilized and prayed. The garden certainly looked different with its arches of bleached wood. Red paving stones gleamed when I ran the sprinkler in the mornings and evenings. We had added a stone angel, a fairy (maybe an elf) reading a book, a sundial, chairs, and a birdbath.

You can work at something for such a long time and get so used to being disappointed that when there are changes, you hardly see them. One spring, I suddenly realized the tarragon plant was huge. In fact, it was no longer a mere plant but a full-grown bush. Thyme and marjoram were a carpet. The lamb's ears had become unstoppable. Robins used the bath and hopped under silver bows of water with an eye out for worms. And there were big, juicy earthworms now, not just centipedes.

I started a daily ritual of taking a glass of lemonade and a book out to the garden to sit and read and soak up the scents and colors. Now and then I dozed. It was easy to pray there, easy to take a pen and paper and write. It amazed me that such flat, hard earth could turn into something that fed my spirit so richly.

Yet even now the entirety of the garden has not completely returned to life. There are still some stubborn patches at the northern end that are resisting rejuvenation. But I have faith that in time the green world will again have its way. Every "springing time" — the old English expression for the season of new birth — this square of soil will be a little bit different, not just because of what I do, but especially because of what I cannot do. The plants are holding their own and casting their seed. Growth has already surprised me in places I did not expect it to be. Root systems are spreading flowers and herbs where the clay thought it could never be disturbed. Shasta daisies are leapfrogging from one spot to another.

Yes, I had a part in it, my family had a part in it, the bees certainly had a part in it — but the greater part none of us had anything to do with. For a while, our hoses can provide the rain (though we can never soak the earth quite as well as a cloud-burst!), but I cannot give the warmth that is necessary, nor the light. I can coax life by adding nitrogen and bonemeal, but I cannot make life. To do so is beyond me. Still, we do what we can. The dirt will be under my nails next spring, and no matter what the other plants have been doing on their own, so far they have not offered up any rosemary. I will see what I can do.

TWO

Gardening," says Thomas Berry, the American ecologist, "is an active participation in the deepest mysteries of the universe." That—and an active participation in the Deepest Mystery of the universe himself.

"I am the true vine," Jesus states a few hours before his arrest in Gethsemane and subsequent execution outside the walls of Jerusalem, "and my Father is the gardener" (John 15:1). He affirms what we have known since Genesis, that by whatever other grandiose names we may know him, God is still a gardener, deity close to the earth. How close? Well, you can't get any closer than flesh and blood. Jesus, like us humans, is flesh and blood and bone, deity from the ground up. He died like humans die and was buried like humans are buried. In that sense, it's appropriate that Mary Magdalene saw him not only as the gardener but also as the flesh-and-blood gardener. It's also appropriate that Jesus calls himself the vine or the garden from which the rest of us get our spiritual sustenance: "No branch can bear fruit by itself; it must remain in the vine. Neither can you bear fruit unless you remain in me" (John 15:4). He is both gardener and garden, both the Creator-Redeemer and the place in which we live and breathe and make something of our lives.

When we talk about Eden, we are talking about him. When

we go to En Gedi, the garden of love, we are going to him. Gethsemane is him—face, hands, and heart. And the Garden Tomb, empty, offers us Jesus as he was always meant to be—and indeed he is us as we were always meant to be.

The accounts of the resurrection of Jesus are somewhat diverse. Why wouldn't they be? How stunned would you be if a person you loved had died and been in the grave for three days and then suddenly walked into your kitchen, brushing dirt off the black suit you buried him in? How long would you be in shock and denial? How much time would it take you to process the impossible? The very fact that John differs from Matthew on small details shows they were each telling the truth as they understood it. If the gospels had been faked, the first thing those instigating the fraud would have done was ensure that each account of Jesus' resurrection dovetailed with the others, like witnesses getting their stories straight before a court appearance. These are real people talking about a real thing that happened, an incredible and incomprehensible event that went beyond anything they had experienced or expected to experience in their lifetimes.

Someone might say, "But Jesus had raised others from the dead." Indeed he had. Lazarus for one, not long before Jesus' own death. The widow of Nain's only son, for another, and Jesus interrupted the funeral procession to do it. Jairus's twelve-year-old daughter for a third, when the mourners laughed at him, "knowing that she was dead" (Luke 8:53), and he merely spoke the Aramaic words *Talitha koum*! "Little girl, I say to you, get up!" —and she did (Mark 5:41).

They had seen him do it. Yes, every disciple had seen the raising of Lazarus and the widow of Nain's son (only Peter, James, and John had witnessed the miracle of the raising of Jairus's daughter). But it is one thing to see the miracle maker produce such miracles, even the unwinding of death; it is another thing when he himself dies. What then? Does that mean that death won? That although the miracle maker could help two or three others, he could do nothing when it came to saving himself? Can a dead man raise the dead? Can a man who is no longer alive command a corpse to breathe?

From the disciples' point of view, and many others, Jesus had been a truly fantastic man, the provider of breathtaking experiences, an extraordinary window to God. But now it was over. Lazarus had better take care of himself. There wouldn't be any more miracles. As humans tend to do when crushing disappointments occur, they became frightened and disillusioned. They withdrew. No doubt some of them reprimanded themselves bitterly for getting pulled into the whole Jesus thing. It had turned out to be too good to be true.

He told them again and again he would rise from the dead. So he did. Consider Mark's words: "[Jesus] then began to teach them that the Son of Man must suffer many things ... and that he must be killed and after three days rise again" (Mark 8:31). Or Luke's, when he quotes Jesus: "The Son of Man must suffer many things ..., and he must be killed and on the third day be raised to life" (Luke 9:22). Or later, when Luke quotes Jesus once more: "We are going up to Jerusalem, and everything that is written by the prophets about the Son of Man will be fulfilled.

He will be delivered over to the Gentiles. They will mock him, insult him and spit on him; they will flog him and kill him. On the third day he will rise again" (Luke 18:31 – 33 TNIV).

But what did all this mean? Was he speaking in code again? Spinning another parable? One day he says he'll rebuild the temple in Jerusalem in three days, and another day he says he'll come back from the dead in three days. What exactly is he saying? How can he do these things? It did not make any sense to them. "The disciples did not understand any of this. Its meaning was hidden from them, and they did not know what he was talking about" (Luke 18:34).

Sunday morning — the sudden end of one world, the astounding beginning of another. A morning beyond belief, totally unexpected and utterly devastating in its impact. Nobody was anticipating it. When those who approached the empty tomb peeked inside, they simply didn't know what they were looking at. They had no categories for it, no vocabulary or theories or theologies to help them get their minds around it. They were overwhelmed. Yes, it was indeed morning at the first day of the world. But Easter, like Christmas, made almost no sense to those who experienced it on the ground.

Angels. One or two? Mark says one, a young man in a white robe sitting on the right inside the empty tomb. Matthew agrees that it's one but says the women saw the stone that sealed the tomb being rolled away and the angel who did it — no ordinary young man; this one had a face like a lightning bolt — sitting on it. Luke has two men in dazzling clothes suddenly appearing at the women's side inside the tomb. John? He has two angels showing up after Peter and John have already been to the tomb and gone, and these angels are sitting inside, one where Jesus' head had been and the other where his feet had been. Only Mary Magdalene sees them.

How can we reconcile these accounts? In Genesis, no matter how many theories abound about how it was done, the main thrust is that God created; God did it. It's the same thing in the gospels concerning the resurrection of Jesus. One angel, two angels; Mary is here, Mary is there. What is the main thrust? *The tomb is empty*; the body is not there. Jesus has been raised from the dead. "Remember," say the angels in Luke, "how he told you" (Luke 24:6). All the gospel accounts agree on this. Each of them take a different track after Sunday morning about which resurrection appearances they are going to concentrate on and how they are going to explain the impact the return of Jesus from the dead had on his followers. But in the garden, among the blue hyacinth and scarlet poppies and white daisies, their focus is the same: The grave is empty. The body is gone. Jesus is alive.

THREE

I'm pretty sure hyacinth and poppies and daisies were decorating the grounds around the tomb. It was a garden, and Mary had no problem imagining she saw a gardener standing behind her: "Thinking he was the gardener, she said, 'Sir, if you have carried him away, tell me where you have put him, and I will get him'" (John 20:15). It was springtime in Israel, and the land would have been brimming with blooming flowers and greening trees at that time of the year. A gardener was not out of place. He was part of the landscape; he was the person who kept everything looking bright and beautiful. He was not an abnormality. He was expected. (Jesus, on the other hand, was an abnormality and was not expected at all.)

Many flowers and plants are native to Israel — the red poppy anemone; the corn poppy (also red); the hyacinth, which has blue flowers; the crown marguerite, which is yellow; the myrtle shrub, which has white blossoms; the mandrake, which produces aromatic yellow fruits in the spring. Who can say which of these, and many others, including various fragrant herbs, were planted or not planted in the grounds around Joseph of Arimathea's personal tomb?

Joseph, a follower of Jesus, was one of the elite, a member of the Council, or Sanhedrin. The tomb itself would be another indicator of his status—well made, cut out of the rock, sealed with a stone like a wheel. And unused. Usually tombs were used repeatedly, and the bones of the dead were gathered up and reburied in an ossuary—an urn or vault for bones—after a full year. The pristine nature of Joseph's tomb is unique. That it was in a garden also makes it special. Kings of Israel were buried in gardens. Manasseh was buried in his palace garden, the garden of Uzza, and so was his son Amon (2 Kings 21:18, 26). The difference between Joseph and these kings is not just the matter of royalty but also the fact that Joseph was "a good and upright man" (Luke 23:50), whereas Manasseh and his son "did evil in the eyes of the LORD" (2 Kings 21:20). Jesus himself then, though he died a criminal's death in the world's eyes and should therefore have been buried without honor, was treated like royalty, his body wrapped in a linen sheet and laid in an expensive, unused tomb in a spring garden.

It's interesting to think about spring being a symbol of Jesus himself long before Gethsemane, Golgotha, and the Garden Tomb. Long before Bethlehem. God created a world rich in allegory that spoke about who he was in a language of stars and comets and tortoises and burros, and about who Jesus was, and about what was going to come and what it all meant. Spring is about new life rising from the dead earth because from the very beginning it was meant to be about Jesus rising from the dead. C. S. Lewis described how the pagan rituals regarding winter and spring symbolized to them the death and resurrection of a god. It caused Lewis to look for the story behind this story, the true story of the death and resurrection of God that was at the heart of it all.

Some like to think Christians borrowed their ideas from religions that had been around for thousands of years. What if it were the other way around? What if the other religions were borrowing from nature symbols about the death and resurrection of Christ that God had placed there from the beginning of time? What if it took Christmas and Easter to make sense of these symbols? What if all nature sings of the Christian God, and the theft of the holy symbols is carried out by those who do not worship him? It may well be that nature is the Son of God's autobiography. Paul wrote, "What may be known about God is plain to them, because God has made it plain to them. For since the creation of the world God's invisible qualities — his eternal power and divine nature — have been clearly seen, being understood from what has been made" (Romans 1:19 – 20). Is the Southern Cross a constellation? A metaphor? An icon? Or all three?

> *The heavens declare the glory of God;*
> *the skies proclaim the work of his hands.*
> *Day after day they pour forth speech;*
> *night after night they display knowledge.*
> *They have no speech, they use no words;*
> *no sound is heard from them.*
> *Yet their voice goes out into all the earth,*
> *their words to the ends of the world.*
>
> Psalm 19:1 – 4 TNIV

Thomas á Kempis, a German monastic, affirms, "If thy heart were right, then every creature would be a mirror of life and a book of holy doctrine. There is no creature so small and abject but it reflects the goodness of God."

The Greek Orthodox novelist and poet Nikos Kazantzakis also weighs in on this theme: "Everything in this world has a hidden meaning, I thought. Men, animals, trees, stars, they are all hieroglyphics. When you see them, you do not understand them. You think they are really men, animals, trees, stars. It is only years later, too late, that you understand."

Finally, William Blake has this to say:

To see a world in a grain of sand
and a Heaven in a wild flower,
hold Infinity in the palm of your hand
and Eternity in an hour.

Fine words — *mirror of life, hieroglyphics, infinity, eternity.* What are these writers getting at? Pretty much the same thing Paul and the Scriptures are getting at: "God's invisible qualities — his eternal power and divine nature — have been clearly seen, being understood from what has been made." Creation is portraiture. And the one sitting for the portrait is a living God.

FOUR

So what happens if we speculate that Jesus is the very embodiment of spring? What does this mean? If God the Creator fashioned the seasons around the divinity of Jesus, what else is crafted to fit? Mountains? The seas? Snowflakes? Tiger sharks and black panthers and blue herons? If Jesus is both gardener and garden, both human and divine, both Creator and Redeemer, what is he not? Is he all? Is the universe held together by his blood and his breath, the cosmos linked by the grasp of his fingers, the galaxies by the light of his mind? Where does it stop?

> The Son is the image of the invisible God, the firstborn over all creation. For in him all things were created: things in heaven and on earth, visible and invisible, whether thrones or powers or rulers or authorities; all things have been created through him and for him. He is before all things, and in him all things hold together.
>
> Colossians 1:15 – 17 TNIV

Jesus is born again out of the cool dark of Joseph's grave. His human body is not limited as it was before his death. He passes through walls, yet he is not a ghost: "While they were still talking about this, Jesus himself stood among them and said to them, 'Peace be with you.' They were startled and frightened, thinking they saw a ghost. He said to them, 'Why are you troubled ...? Touch me and see; a ghost does not have flesh and bones, as you see I have'" (Luke 24:36 – 39). Compare Luke's account to how Jesus passes through locked doors in John's gospel (20:19, 26).

As Mary discovered in the garden and two others discovered on the road to Emmaus, Jesus was not readily recognizable. It was Jesus all right, but he looked different. At Emmaus he blessed the bread, broke it, and gave it to his companions: "Then their eyes were opened and they recognized him .... They asked each other, 'Were not our hearts burning within us while he talked with us on the road and opened the Scriptures to us?'" (Luke 24:31 – 32). He could vanish from people's sight in the blink of an eye (24:31). Cover long distances in a finger snap (24:33 – 36). He ascended to heaven in this astonishing body (24:51). Clearly the human who walks through the garden to talk to Mary is altered from the human who died. Indeed, this human is unlike any human who has walked on the earth before or since.

In Romans, Paul writes, "Those God foreknew he also predestined to be conformed to the image of his Son, that he might be the firstborn among many brothers and sisters" (8:29 TNIV). In his second letter to the church at Corinth, Paul declares essentially the same thing: "We all, who with unveiled faces contemplate the Lord's glory, are being transformed into his image with ever-increasing glory" (2 Corinthians 3:18 TNIV). In his letter to the church at Ephesus, he is more explicit: "... until we all reach unity in the faith and in the knowledge of the Son of

God and become mature, attaining to the whole measure of the fullness of Christ" (Ephesians 4:13). We are being changed into his image. What sort of image?

In his first letter to the Christians living in Corinth, Paul had argued that Jesus was a second Adam and that in the same way we shared the first Adam's natural body we would share the second Adam's spiritual body: "Just as we have borne the image of the earthly man, so shall we bear the image of the heavenly man" (1 Corinthians 15:49 TNIV). He goes on to describe how, at the resurrection of the dead, believers will suddenly have the same body Jesus had at his resurrection:

> Listen, I tell you a mystery: We will not all sleep, but we will all be changed—in a flash, in the twinkling of an eye, at the last trumpet. For the trumpet will sound, the dead will be raised imperishable, and we will be changed. For the perishable must clothe itself with the imperishable, and the mortal with immortality.
>
> 1 Corinthians 15:51–53

This much is clear. The body of Jesus that Mary saw in the garden will be like the body all believers will have. Jesus "will transform our lowly bodies so that they will be like his glorious body" (Philippians 3:21). What else? In his letter to the church at Colossae, Paul writes:

> Do not lie to each other, since you have taken off your old self with its practices and have put on the new self, which is being renewed in knowledge in the image of

its Creator. Here there is no Gentile or Jew, circumcised or uncircumcised, barbarian, Scythian, slave or free, but Christ is all, and is in all.

Colossians 3:9 – 11

We are talking about more than having the same body now. We are talking about what goes on inside—a new nature with new practices, a renewed *imago dei* to replace the old *imago dei* damaged at Eden. It is not just about a new human body but a new human soul, an *imago christus*. In fact, we are talking about a new civilization. All are equal, and old labels and old terms are discarded. Earth is to be one race, one nation of believers. Earth as a whole is meant to be like this, not just bits and pieces of it, one village here, one town there, one country here, one denomination there. Christ's resurrection has created the possibility of a redeemed global humanity, and despite all our diversity, it is unity and equality that are to be paramount. "You are a chosen people," says Peter—"... a holy nation," he emphasizes (1 Peter 2:9). "God's special possession .... Once you were not a people; but now you are the people of God" (2:9 – 10 TNIV).

So in Christ Jesus you are all children of God through faith, for all of you who were baptized into Christ have clothed yourselves with Christ. There is neither Jew nor Gentile, neither slave nor free, neither male nor female, for you are all one in Christ Jesus.

Galatians 3:26 – 28 TNIV

Those who believe in Jesus are meant to be this new

humanity, this new race, this new civilization. They are meant to be one in Christ Jesus. Just as it was in Eden in the beginning. The Garden Tomb has given us a new creation, or rather, a renewed creation. "If anyone is in Christ, the new creation has come: The old has gone, the new is here!" (2 Corinthians 5:17 TNIV). Not just inside one person who believes, but all around—wherever people believe—since all who believe are one in Christ. There really is meant to be a new heaven and a new earth (Revelation 21:1). "Neither circumcision nor uncircumcision means anything; what counts is a new creation" (Galatians 6:15).

FIVE

Just before our son was born, my wife and I looked at black-and-white images of him on an ultrasound monitor. It was wonderful, of course, watching him move around and kick his legs and turn his head. But what a difference when he came bursting out of the womb into the full light of day! Pink skin, ten fingers and ten toes, eyes, lips, a body we could hold, cheeks we could kiss, a cry of his own—we were ecstatic.

We had the same experience with our daughter. The grainy black-and-white images of her twisting and turning in the womb were great, but it paled in comparison to seeing her in living color and holding her little body in our hands and kissing the top of her beautiful head. Moving from the ultrasound to the real thing was like going from night to day.

This is what happens when a person believes in the risen Christ. You move from dark to light, from dim images of reality to bright clarity, from a kind of twilight zone to a morning streaming with sunshine. It was certainly that way with me. Not raised in a Christian home, having no spiritual instruction at all, I experienced Christ bursting in on me when I was thirteen like a comet blazing a path through the dark heavens.

No one taught me to pray. I just began to kneel by my bed and pray. No one taught me to read the Bible; no one even gave me one. I found my father's blue Gideon New Testament, the one he had been given when he served in the Air Force during the Second World War, opened it up and began to read. I can remember to this day the feeling of peace that surged over me like a wave of cool water when I prayed, I can remember finding in that small New Testament things Jesus said that filled me with a brilliant light and a soaring joy. No one talked me into feeling those things; I simply felt them. I flew with the wings of eagles. For me, it really was like being born a second time; it really was like being raised from the dead. When I emerged from my baptism and stood there in front of hundreds of people, water streaming from my head and face, I felt as though I was shining like a thousand sparkling diamonds.

A new body in Christ. A new person in Christ. A new humanity in Christ. Is there any other gift Jesus brings with him from the black of Joseph's tomb? Paul writes to the Christians at Ephesus, "You were taught, with regard to your former way of life, to put off your old self, which is being corrupted by its deceitful desires; to be made new in the attitude of your minds; and to put on the new self, created to be like God in true righteousness and holiness" (Ephesians 4:22–24).

The definition of being like Jesus expands even further. The new human, the new humanity, is to be holy, just as God is holy. An old commandment— "Be holy because I, the LORD your God, am holy" (Leviticus 19:2) —but now a new possibility. Peter lines up with Paul when he writes that the new humans are supposed to be a holy nation. But he presses the definition of the new human even further:

His divine power has given us everything we need for a
godly life through our knowledge of him who called us
by his own glory and goodness. Through these he has
given us his very great and precious promises, so that
through them you may participate in the divine nature,
having escaped the corruption in the world caused by
evil desires.

2 Peter 1:3–4 TNIV

J. B. Phillips translates, "It is through [Christ] that God's
greatest and most precious promises have become available to us
men, making it possible for you to escape the inevitable disin-
tegration that lust produces in the world and to share in God's
essential nature," or, as the REB puts it, "to share in the very
being of God."

This is big news. Incredible but almost frightening—to
participate in the divine nature, to share in God's essential
nature, to come to share in the very being of God. Paul told us
in Romans 1:20 that from the beginning, God's self-expression,
something of God's very character, could be glimpsed in what
he had made—lightning, mountain peaks, killer whales, eagles,
even humans. Now Peter is telling us that whatever was true
about the old *imago dei* is surpassed by the new.

It is not just that the handiwork of God can be seen in us.
The death and resurrection of Christ have put God himself
inside us. We will not be God. But his divine nature will increasingly become unmistakable in our words and deeds. Not because
we have made it so, but because *he* has made it so. We believers,
from the broken and warring human race, will radiate God's

core just as the very bowels of the star that is our sun pours out the brightest light and intense, blazing heat. To be in Christ's image has come to mean to be in God's image, since Christ and the Father are one (John 10:30).

And to be in God's image means far more than possessing an astonishing body or a new spirit or being a fresh human race. God, who made the galaxies, lives in those who believe in the risen Christ. God, who made the red macaws and the green pythons and the majestic grizzly, lives in those who believe in the risen Christ. God, who made sunrise, sunset, and all the lightning-faced angels, lives in those who believe in the risen Christ.

The Creator lives in the believer. The Redeemer. The Lover. The One who was there for the human race at Eden, at Gethsemane, at the Garden Tomb. Eternity lives in the believer. Not just by the piece—the *whole of God* thrives in the daughters and sons who believe. I AM dwells in those who worship the risen Christ.

Theosis, Gregory Palamas calls it, *divinization*, becoming partakers of the divine nature. A mystery that is a reality, the incomprehensible in an ordinary woman or ordinary man's face and soul. Not becoming the eternal, all-powerful, and unique Lord of heaven and earth, but *sharing in his divine nature*. "You will be like God" (Genesis 3:5)—the lie of Eden a surprising truth of the Garden Tomb.

You often get the sense that the apostles themselves scarcely knew the full ramifications of what they were inspired to write and speak. The truth grasped them, they grasped him, but many times, perhaps, just the hem of Jesus' garment was in the grip of their spirit and intellect. We are being transformed more and more into what Jesus is like, writes Paul to the Corinthians. But he is compelled to push the envelope even further in his letter to the Ephesians. He remarks that the day will come when the unity the new faith promises will inevitably occur and with it a unity in our comprehension of Jesus. This will be a maturing process, but when it is consummated, we will have attained to the "whole measure of the fullness of Christ" (Ephesians 4:13). "Real maturity," J. B. Phillips calls it. "His very breath and blood flow through us," writes Eugene Peterson (Ephesians 4:16 MSG).

What does it mean that one day we will attain "to the whole measure of the fullness of Christ"? It means that humanity was created to be human, not created to be God, but that the very pinnacle of achievement of our race is *to be like Jesus*. And in becoming like Jesus, we will share a part of God's nature. Only God will be God. But only those who believe in the risen Christ will be God's children.

It is not as though we achieve this by the force of our own will or by our own grit and determination. It is a grace. The fruits of every biblical garden are a grace. Just as it is not necessary to know how an apple helps your body for you to benefit from eating it, so it is not necessary to comprehend fully the way God blesses us in order to benefit from that blessing. All we need to do is take the blessing into our spirit by an act of faith. We simply believe, with whatever belief we can muster, and so draw into the throat and stomach and blood of our soul the stunning implications of the resurrection of Jesus Christ from the dead. Often we act much more like the father who wants Jesus to heal his son than a mortal becoming immortal and glittering with God. Nevertheless, our human and divine natures are not always opposed, and in the desperate father's prayer are twins joined at the hip in a relationship that will not vanish before we put on our immortal bodies: "I do believe; help me overcome my unbelief!" (Mark 9:24).

SIX

I have always found deeply moving the ceremonies where ashes are scattered. Cremation itself has never bothered me. Many North Americans are more comfortable placing a body in the ground and holding on to a memory of their loved one intact and whole. Of course, the truth is that body also goes from "ashes to ashes and dust to dust"; it just does it more slowly.

My father always thought too much land was being wasted on graveyards. "The land can be used for planting seeds instead of bodies," he said. "It can be used to put up buildings instead of tombstones, to put up houses for the poor that will keep them out of the wind and rain." So after Mother died, the day came when he and I went to the funeral home to pick up her ashes.

Funeral home workers must always show an attitude of empathy and solemnity. But I will never forget the moment the man who was helping us brought a cardboard carton out of the back and placed it in my hands. His face was like chalk. Even though he had probably done this a hundred times, handing a son his mother's ashes had not become an emotionless ritual for him. And the young secretary who sat behind a desk oozed genuine sympathy from her dark eyes.

There were four plain copper urns in the box. The weight of the ashes surprised me — I had not thought they would be so heavy. I carried the box with the urns down the busy street, walking side by side with father. We had walked together many times when I'd been a boy, placing my feet in his boot prints as we marched through deep snow to the dentist; striding back from Christmas dinner at a fancy restaurant, two or three miles from home, the temperature 40 below and the frost stinging our cheeks; scrounging around a field at night for scrap wood to use in our furnace. But this was a different walk, unlike any other we had taken before. While all around us, people rushed in and out of shops, drove cars swiftly through yellow lights, called out to each other, and whistled and laughed, it was as though we passed through all this activity on another road, one that bypassed the stuff of earth and took us straight toward the skyline of eternity.

In time, I took a similar walk, carrying the ashes of my father. Now two urns rest side by side on one of the bookcases in the room in which I do a good deal of my writing. I have taken some of the ashes out of each and mingled them with the soil in my garden. I'm not sure what I thought the ashes should look like—they were white and black and grey, just like the ashes I take out of my woodstove. But the weight felt different. Eternity always feels different. Even if it does not seem like eternity at the time.

SEVEN

So much of the life of faith seems to exist in another place. "When you die," we are told, "then you will live. Later, on the other side, you will understand. Tomorrow, when God decides it is the right time, you will know why that prayer was not answered. In heaven, you will see your mother again, you will see your daughter, you will see your husband." So much of Christianity appears to pin its hopes on a never-never land of the soul.

It is not just Christianity, of course. A concern about life after death has been with all races and cultures from as far back as we can find evidence of human life. But Christianity is reckless. First it claims that we had paradise once and lost it. Then it claims that God came among us in human form to set things right and that we killed him. Then it tells us that God came back to life. Then it tells us that we will share in God's divine nature. It's a lot to take in.

Much is in those who believe.

Almost too much. A new body, a new spirit, a new world, God himself. Can we really take it all in? What difference does it make if we do? We still suffer, still have unanswered prayers, still run short on cash, still have heart disease. We have a wonderful time at church, singing and praying and worshiping; two hours later, the glow is gone, and we are quarreling with our best friend. Or a phone call devastates us with the news that someone we love is dead. How does the Garden Tomb alter the tragedies and dislocations that saturate our lives?

We could say there is a certain comfort in believing there is life after death. And this is true. The hope of heaven will always be an encouragement to Christians who have lost people they love. This is a hope, of course, that is common ground for everyone now. Modern humanity does not see any need for Jesus' death and resurrection in order to guarantee immortality. Immortality appears to have become a given. There are those who still maintain that death is no more than a hole in the ground or the hot fires of cremation. But the greater portion of the global community takes it for granted that the gift of eternity is open to all, and attendance at a variety of funeral services will reveal that this approach to death and tragedy is almost universal.

The irony is that for a number of Christians, particularly in North America, heaven has become marginalized. It is a fringe belief. Christians know they are supposed to believe in it, and so they do. But what is much more important to them is heaven on earth. Not the kind that opens the gate to the Second Eden, a world of unity and harmony and love centered in the Father, Son, and Holy Spirit; no, their idea of heaven on earth is material wealth, creaturely comforts, good health and longevity, and the more of it the better. The "heaven not yet" is vague and unknown, a somewhat frightening country that still requires death in order to take part in its wonders and colors. "Heaven right here," on the other hand, offers Father, Son, and Holy Spirit, all the people and food and movies you love, and no chill of death. It only makes sense to try to enjoy it for as long as possible.

Death has a way of showing up uninvited, however. It is then that a typical North American Christian suddenly takes "heaven not yet" seriously because their own glass bubble on earth has been shattered—and it's true for those who aren't Christians too. Questions about eternity and the survival of the soul no longer take a backseat. Existence on earth is not as safe and friendly as it once was. It has shown us its fangs. We become emigrants of the spirit who seek a better country, a fairer land to which we can travel and set down new roots. Pain and suffering have a way of jolting our priorities and belief systems. They make us desperate enough to stake everything on a dangerous voyage to a new world from which no one has ever returned.

Heaven fell into disrepute in the nineteenth and twentieth centuries. It was not rational. It could not be proven. It was the drug of the human race. The hope of heaven kept people from working to improve their situation on earth. Now heaven is here and not there. Now we work very hard to improve the situation on earth. An idyllic never-never land does not matter.

Until the skull of death leers. Then some of us find our way to The Place of the Skull. Which takes us to a garden in a graveyard and a mourner named Mary, who is weeping, as we have so often wept in our own graveyards. There we meet a person who has returned from the far country. He says he has carried the sins of the world on his back. All the spilled blood and wickedness. The scorching tears and crushed hearts. All the black despair. All hell, all judgment. The things no one seems to take seriously anymore. "Peace be with you," this Jesus says. "Put your finger here; see my hands. Reach out your hand and put it into my side. Stop doubting and believe" (John 20:26–27).

Some believe; some do not. There are, after all, competitors that clamor for our attention — and not just other religions. Thousands claim to have had near-death or after-death experiences. They have written books and appeared on television talk shows and set up websites online. They have seen a light at the end of a dark tunnel, they say. They have seen angels. They have seen the skies of heaven. Coming back to life, some have turned to Christ, and others have not. Yet for all that has been written along these lines, there is no one yet who has been dead and buried for three days and lived to talk about it — except Jesus.

But we miss the point if we confine the impact of Jesus' resurrection to what does or does not happen to us after death. The picture painted in the Passover garden is much bigger than that. The first Christians, men and women who had seen Jesus live and die, were not stupefied by the knowledge, content to sit in a corner somewhere and pine for heaven. They were galvanized into action. Fear of death and fear of life vanished. They crossed continents and oceans with strong news — declaring that not only was Jesus' message unique, Jesus himself was unique. His words about who he was and who we were had been corroborated by his return from the dead. Not only was life after death possible; life before death was possible too. Human existence was revitalized by the Christ in the garden. If he came back from the dead to nail down eternal life for those who wanted it, then that life had begun *now*, for eternity was timeless. It was not just a tomorrow country anymore. Eternity was now. It was in everyone who believed.

The first Christians still looked forward to being with Jesus in heaven. But they also looked forward to being with him on earth. They were excited about dying and being with Christ. But they were also excited about living and being with Christ. Christ's resurrection was meant not to deflate human life but to expand it. Not to restrict it to a distant date when death would return our souls to God but to throw it wide open so that every living day would return our souls to God. The resurrection of Jesus fleshed out human life. It did not spiritualize it. He came back body and soul and redeemed both, made both equally significant. Not just for later. For now. Beginning with the present. "I have come that they may have life," Jesus says, "and have it to the full" (John 10:10).

Jesus means to put that spring garden in us. All the colors, all the scents, all the textures—he means to fill eyes and nostrils of dust as well as spirit. There is no waiting for heaven if heaven is within, no groaning for a better life if the better life has begun. Christians lead an existence in two locations—in heaven and on earth. And when they die, they are not dead.

What brings color to the blood is that faith is a current event. It impacts our marriages, our children, our careers, our recreation. It is not dull stuff. It is God set loose. All of a sudden, we are running to catch up. Christ has risen from the dead, and this means I am different. This means the world is different, and the difference is good. If we believe it, nothing is pointless again. Even the darkness is streaked with light.

PART FIVE

SECOND EDEN

The GARDEN of the NEW WORLD

On each side of the river stood the tree of life,
bearing twelve crops of fruit,
yielding its fruit every month.
Revelation 22:2

ONE

There was once a woman with skin like mahogany who lived alone in a little house with a dog and a cat and a blue-breasted songbird. She had tea in the morning and warm milk with cinnamon at night. Far out in the country she lived, and though a road curled around her house before rushing over a small green hill, very few people ever walked along it. Now and then, a weary traveler would stop at her door, however, and she was always eager to give them warm broth, some cider from her apple tree, and sturdy vegetables from her garden.

She was proud of her garden. Peas and strawberries grew in it, green beans and rhubarb, carrots and plums and peaches. A white fence wrapped itself around the rows, and a gate that latched and unlatched let her in and out. "Thank you, God, for my garden," she often said. "My dog loves the peas, the cat eats the strawberries, my songbird loves the corn, and I am fond of hoeing between the rows and putting red carnations in a glass jar by my bed."

Her tranquil world was shattered one day when a group of soldiers in dark cloaks rode up to her door, holding torches of fire. "We need meat!" roared their leader, who had a red beard that fell to his toes. "Cook us up some meat, and we will spare your house. For we have orders from the king to burn this land

and all its buildings because you treacherous peasants are plotting against him."

"I have no meat, "said the woman. "But look, you are welcome to my corn and beets and all my fresh green apples."

"Corn! Beets! Apples!" railed the leader. "What do you take us for? A pack of goats? We are the king's men, and we will have meat. If you will not give us your meat, we will burn your house to the ground."

"Alas, I have no meat," said the woman, "but you are welcome to cheese and bread and cider, as much as you and your men need."

"Cheese, eh?" snorted the leader. "If you have cheese, then you must have a goat or a cow. Where are they?"

"I don't know," answered the woman. "They wander the hills at will."

"Track them down!" roared the leader to his men. "When you find them, bring them here, and we will slaughter them and fill our stomachs with their roasted flesh!"

Now the woman's dog was no ordinary dog, and the woman's cat was no ordinary cat. Upon hearing these words, they raced into the hills ahead of the soldiers and warned the goat and the cow.

In fact, they led them to a secret cave, the opening to which no human eye could detect. For hours, the soldiers scoured the hills, galloping from one meadow to another. But though they found the tracks of the cow and goat, as soon as they tried to follow them, they found themselves riding in circles and bumping into one another.

At dusk they returned to their leader and reported that the animals could not be found.

"Sorcery!" yelled the leader in a fury. "Witchcraft! Bind the woman and place her inside the house and burn it down around her ears!"

The woman was tied up and left in the house while the men began to set fire to the thatched roof. The soldiers rode their horses back and forth through the garden until every plant was broken and every vegetable ground into the dirt. Then they hacked down the fruit trees and set them ablaze. The house an orange volcano, the soldiers and their leaders streamed down the road and away, their torches trailing green sparks, their shouts of rage ringing through the night air.

But the woman did not die. The cat unlatched the back door, and the dog bit into the rope and dragged the woman to safety. The goat arrived and chewed through the knots, and the cow's warm milk filled the woman with fresh strength. But she could not put out the fire. During the night, a thin moon shone on smoking coals and a ravaged garden. Only the gate of the picket fence stood, all by itself. None of them could find the blue-breasted songbird.

The morning revealed a horizon to the west filled with black smoke. "Ah, alas," cried the woman, sinking to her knees, "they have destroyed the land. How will those poor people survive? My God, what will you do to help us?" But God did not speak.

The woman wept and wandered around her yard, her animals weeping and trailing after her. Everything was black with soot. Suddenly the woman stumbled over something. Glancing down, she gave a cry of joy and snatched up her hoe. The soldiers had not destroyed it, and the fire had not scorched it. "My God," said the woman, "if you help me, I can start again." But God did not speak.

She went ahead and hoed the ground all the same. In time, she rebuilt the fence, and from the hair the goat lent her, she wove a tent. It was still midsummer, and the woman decided she would try to grow a second garden.

"My God," she said, "if you help me, I can grow food and take it to the people who live over the hill and underneath the smoke." God stood by the gate to the garden, but she did not see him.

The four animals did and knelt. "What on earth are you doing?" the woman asked them as she paused to observe the spectacle. But they gave no answer, and she saw nothing, so she continued to hoe the scorched earth.

That night, God sent an angel to sow the soil, another to water it, another to make it grow. In the morning, the woman saw that the garden was green and full. Corn towered, tomatoes were ripe on their vines, a plum tree was purple with fruit.

"My God," shouted the woman in joy, "look what you have done!" She took a basket she had woven from reeds that grew by a creek and filled it with fruit and vegetables, as well as cheese from the goat and the cow. She thought, "I will take this to the people on the other side of the hill, and when the basket is empty, I will come back and fill it again." She set out on the road, and the dog and the cat and the goat and the cow followed her.

But the dog kept looking back over his shoulder and whining. "What is it?" she asked him, but she did not stop, nor did she turn around. She was almost to the foot of the hill before a tomato vine slipped past her and over the hilltop, bright red with clusters of fat tomatoes.

To her left, a great bunch of pea plants laden with pea pods hurried past. She stopped and shrieked with delight as mounds of green-leafed potato plants broke open the soil between her feet and leaped over the hill, throwing clods of earth to the left and the right. Apple trees sprouted like grass, and when she blinked, she missed the emergence of a peach orchard. Pumpkins on their vines rumbled past, and rows of carrots marched to the horizon, their tops swaying like feathers. She sat down on the road on top of one of the potato plants, and her animals sat with her. All day, her garden raced out of sight — tall corn walking, heads of lettuce rolling, red beets spinning like tops. Finally she got to her feet and climbed to the top of the hill to look.

Every place she looked was alive with plants and trees. Black coals and charred ruins vanished into green as cabbage and spinach and turnips took over. And daisies came on the scene too. And peonies. And carnations. And tulips. The foliage became rainbows of berries and flowers and vegetables, and among the arches of the rainbows she saw men and women and children bending down in wonder to pick strawberries and beans and dig up sweet potatoes.

"Thank you," she whispered to her God.

The five of them — woman, goat, cow, cat, dog — turned around and walked back to her home. The woman's garden was still there, but it had spilled over the top of the fence and wriggled and rustled as if it were a wild animal. It was the center of a green star that radiated north, east, south, and west. All day and all night it grew in all directions. For weeks, this went on. Then months.

One morning, the wriggling and rustling stopped. The woman came out of her tent—a cherry tree spotted with fruit had grown over it during the night—and stood with her animals hip-deep in kale. All was quiet, every plant still. The garden had filled the land as far as she could see. Hummingbirds hummed. Ladybugs flickered past her nose. In the hush she could hear the distant clop of horses' hooves.

Her first instinct was to run and hide, but she held back. Her dog's tail was wagging so hard it was going in circles. She looked up the road and saw seven riders in gold and white armor coming toward her from the direction of the small hill (which had become a forest of apple trees). A blue-breasted bird perched on the shoulder of a man with long silver hair. Suddenly it flew to the goat and cow and dog and cat and landed on the woman's arm and began to sing.

The riders dismounted. "It is the sign we have been looking for," said the man with silver hair. "This must be your bird."

"Yes," exclaimed the woman with joy. "I have not seen her since the soldiers with the torches of fire came."

One of the riders, a woman with hair like the sun, said, "They will not come again."

A man with a closely trimmed white beard stood looking at the garden within the picket fence. "The ancient books said the garden would begin in such a humble enclosure."

"And that a bluebird would reveal the garden's source," added the woman with sun hair.

"I only hoed the ground," the woman with mahogany skin told them. "All the rest the garden did on its own!"

"Do not be afraid," said the sun woman. "What has happened is a good thing."

"Do you know how far the garden has grown?" asked the woman with mahogany skin, the blue-breasted bird now perched on her arm.

The white-bearded man bent low and looked deep into her eyes. "M'lady," he said, with surprise in his voice, "it covers the earth."

The seven of them stayed with the woman that night. At dawn, they rose and invited her to join them. They wished to take her to meet the king. "The true king," said the sun woman. "He will probably ask you to live at the palace."

"But my home is here by the garden," said the woman.

"So it is," smiled the white-bearded man. "And it is as fine a place as any. Indeed, it is fit for a king. He will want to come to you here. Wait for him." The seven rode over the hill of apples, and the woman waited, tending her garden, cooking simple meals, every now and then glancing at the horizon—until one morning soldiers of white and gold, flashing like fire, rode out of the sunrise.

The soldiers built her a new home, not small, not large, just right. She slept in it each night, thankful for its warmth and shelter. In the mornings, she rose and ate strawberries and cherries and drank tea before heading out to work the soil and care for the plants. At night, she drank a mug of warm milk and thought about the good God who gave her such a good life—and about the good king she had never met.

But then one day the king did come to her garden. The warm milk of the cow gave him a white moustache. It seemed he could not get enough of the cherries. And her laughter and his laughter made the blue-breasted songbird circle and wheel overhead like a gull.

The visit was long. Some say he is there yet, just over the small hill forested with green apple trees, at the heart of the garden that has become the world.

TWO

I grew up in a large city, but we lived at the edge of it. The buses didn't drive out to our subdivision because it was too rural. There was a thick forest across the street, actually two, and we called them First Forest and Second Forest. In between them was a marsh spiked with cattails. Mallards landed in the marsh every autumn. Deer and rabbits darted in and out of the woods year-round. We weren't urban; we were semi-urban. We weren't rural; we were semi-rural. My brother and sister and I were children in two worlds.

In time, the trees were cut down. I remember the holocaust of earth ripped up by bulldozers and piles of burning stumps that smoked for weeks. The city was getting an international airport. The interest a boy has in bright silver aircraft did not alleviate the dismay I felt as I walked through the dirt and ashes. Everything was now horizontal. There would be no more ducks or geese and no more deer. The tall green was ended.

People planted their own trees. The now-bald prairie was forested by front lawns. Dad put birch in our yard. Everyone had flowers, of course—peonies and rosebushes and snapdragons, which did well in the prairie summer heat as long as they had lots of water. In the backyards were vegetable gardens—some small, some large. They were pleasant and ordinary. Except for one.

At the north end of our block lived an Italian family. (I mentioned this family earlier when we talked about Eden.) Their entire backyard was a garden, not just on the horizontal but on the vertical and the diagonal. It was as if they had created another dimension. They had no children for us to play with; the man and woman were older. They had bought the house and retired there, and the garden was their pleasure. I only saw her in it once; the rest of the time it was him. Short, dark hue of skin, smiling, always friendly, always ready to talk. When I was about to travel to Europe and spend the summer in Italy, he explained his home country to me at some length. I can only remember his warning that the citizens of Naples were thieves. But it was said gently and with a touch of humor. It was when I returned that I christened him Mister Buon Giorno, Mister Good Morning.

You may remember that every plant in his garden seemed to have enormous, thick, dark leaves, as though his backyard enjoyed a tropical climate. Cucumbers were either perfectly tiny and just right for pickles, or else they were huge — barely smaller than baseball bats. Beans — green and yellow and scarlet — peas in their pods, carrot tops like bushes. Mister Buon Giorno grew things no one else attempted. Broccoli and cauliflower were there, and the purple sheen of eggplant. There was a grapevine — probably of Italian wine grapes, for all I know — a plum tree, a pear tree. And a friend once swore he saw Mister Buon Giorno harvesting apricots and figs. I am certain there were no palm trees, nor did I see any pineapples, coconuts, or bananas — though frankly, I don't think it would have surprised me to have discovered them there. But it was not what he grew so much as how much of it he grew and how strong and dark was the green blood that ran through each plant.

His garden touched the clouds. It was a second Garden of Eden. As in the story of Jack, the beanstalks were trees that dwarfed the poles to which they had been tied. The tomatoes were fat, red baseballs. The corncobs were canary yellow and thick. His harvest baskets overflowed. A colony of bees covered the blossoms. Birds flocked to the tunnels of arched leaves close to the soil. The rich brew of growth pricked our nostrils. The sun always shone.

He is gone, and with him the garden, and I haven't had any occasion to return to the street of my youth since my father's death. But I don't think there is a time I am in any garden that I don't find myself thinking back to that garden and the man who tended it. Suppose everything grew like that. Suppose every backyard was that full and that high with plants. Suppose that in all that color and life, the human race were to find contentment. I imagine Mister Buon Giorno is smiling somewhere and tapping another high pole into the ground. Good enough for earth, good enough for heaven.

THREE

Exiled from Eden, we have always wanted it back. The garden of love at En Gedi confirmed this. The Messiah in Gethsemane and the Garden Tomb finally made our return definite. God's words had painted a picture for thousands of years of the kind of world the Messiah would bring in. Whatever else it would be—and it would be many things—it most certainly would be a new garden.

> *A shoot will come up from the stump of Jesse;*
> *from his roots a Branch will bear fruit....*
>
> *He will not judge by what he sees with his eyes,*
> *or decide by what he hears with his ears;*
> *but with righteousness he will judge the needy,*
> *with justice he will give decisions for the poor of the earth.*
> *He will strike the earth with the rod of his mouth;*
> *with the breath of his lips he will slay the wicked.*
> *Righteousness will be his belt*
> *and faithfulness the sash around his waist.*
>
> *The wolf will live with the lamb,*
> *the leopard will lie down with the goat,*
> *the calf and the lion and the yearling together;*
> *and a little child will lead them.*

The cow will feed with the bear,
    their young will lie down together,
    and the lion will eat straw like the ox.
The infant will play near the hole of the cobra,
    and the young child will put his hand into the viper's nest.
They will neither harm nor destroy
    on all my holy mountain,
for the earth will be filled with the knowledge of the LORD
    as the waters cover the sea.

                    Isaiah 11:1, 3–9

Righteousness and equality come with the Messiah. So does a garden setting where carnivores return to the eating habits of Eden: "To all the beasts of the earth and all the birds of the air and all the creatures that move on the ground—everything that has the breath of life in it—I give every green plant for food" (Genesis 1:30). The peace in this environment is total. So is the harmony.

For to us a child is born,
    to us a son is given,
    and the government will be on his shoulders.
And he will be called
    Wonderful Counselor, Mighty God,
    Everlasting Father, Prince of Peace.
Of the increase of his government and peace
    there will be no end.
He will reign on David's throne
    and over his kingdom,

> *establishing and upholding it*
> *with justice and righteousness*
> *from that time on and forever.*
>
> Isaiah 9:6−7

The imagery of garden and oasis is never far from these prophecies of the coming reign of the Messiah over the entire earth:

> *See, a king will reign in righteousness*
> *and rulers will rule with justice.*
> *Each man will be like a shelter from the wind*
> *and a refuge from the storm,*
> *like streams of water in the desert*
> *and the shadow of a great rock in a thirsty land.*
>
> Isaiah 32:1−2

Nor is it only the prophecies of Isaiah that speak of the Eden to come. Hosea has words that foretell it, and Micah, and Zechariah:

> *In that day I will make a covenant for [Israel]*
> *with the beasts of the field, the birds of the air*
> *and the creatures that move along the ground.*
> *Bow and sword and battle*
> *I will abolish from the land,*
> *so that all may lie down in safety.*
>
> Hosea 2:18

> *He will judge between many peoples*
> *and will settle disputes for strong nations far and wide.*

They will beat their swords into plowshares
and their spears into pruning hooks.
Nation will not take up sword against nation,
nor will they train for war anymore.
Every man will sit under his own vine
and under his own fig tree,
and no one will make them afraid,
for the LORD Almighty has spoken.

Micah 4:3–4

Rejoice greatly, Daughter Zion!
Shout, Daughter Jerusalem!
See, your king comes to you,
righteous and having salvation,
lowly and riding on a donkey,
on a colt, the foal of a donkey.
I will take away the chariots from Ephraim
and the warhorses from Jerusalem,
and the battle bow will be broken.
He will proclaim peace to the nations.
His rule will extend from sea to sea
and from the River to the ends of the earth.

Zechariah 9:9–10 TNIV

Hosea makes it clear that the enmity between animals and humans, a corruption that resulted from the fall in Eden, will be ended. Each prophet foretells that war will cease to exist—God's peace will be universal. And Micah emphasizes the garden. People safe and content in their vineyards and under the shade of their fig trees.

Yet it is Ezekiel who sees perhaps most clearly the garden that is to come, for his vision could almost have been lifted directly from Revelation itself (Ezekiel 47:1 – 12). He is shown a river that flows from the temple. This river runs all the way to the Dead Sea and turns it into fresh water, restoring life where before there was only death.

> Swarms of living creatures will live wherever the river flows. There will be large numbers of fish, because this water flows there and makes the salt water fresh; so where the river flows everything will live. . . . Fruit trees of all kinds will grow on both banks of the river. Their leaves will not wither, nor will their fruit fail. Every month they will bear fruit, because the water from the sanctuary flows to them. Their fruit will serve for food and their leaves for healing.
>
> Ezekiel 47:9, 12

We see from the gospels that where the Messiah speaks and heals and blesses, this new world is breaking through. His death and resurrection make it a certainty. His return will make it a reality. The first coming begins the new creation; the second coming completes it. Matthew, Mark, Luke, and John are the planting of the garden and the sowing of the seed; Revelation is the garden fully grown.

FOUR

Many shy away from Revelation's dark images of judgment and destruction. In fact, however, the book is full of the imagery of color and light and song, and its ending is the final garden, hoped for from the moment Eden was lost. Revelation is not only a vision of the ultimate clash between evil and God; it is a vision of a perfect beauty finally and fully realized.

The splendor of Second Eden is preceded by the splendor of the people of God. "Come," an angel says to John, "I will show you the bride, the wife of the Lamb" (Revelation 21:9). He shows John the Holy City, Jerusalem, coming down out of heaven from God (21:10).

The bride shines with the glory of God like a jasper. Jasper is opaque and normally colored red, brown, yellow, or green. The jasper he compares here to the luminescence of the bride is crystal clear (21:11).

The city is built of gold and is as pure as glass (21:18). The streets are gold too, and the city gates are pearls (21:21). The foundations of the city are decorated with precious stones — jasper (red, brown, yellow, or green), sapphire (blue), chalcedony (gray), emerald (green), sardonyx (red and white bands), carnelian (red and yellow), chrysolite (yellow and green), beryl (green, blue, yellow, or white), topaz (golden, yellow and brown, pink or colorless), chrysoprase (apple green), jacinth (blue), and amethyst (purple) (21:19–20).

The twelve gates of the city are inscribed with the names of the twelve tribes of Israel. The city wall has twelve foundation stones engraved with the names of the twelve apostles. The city is the people of God—we already know this because we know the city is the bride of the Lamb—and the people of God are a mix of Jews (the tribes of Israel) and those who are not Jewish (the apostles took the gospel to all races). Revelation is a book crammed with symbols and gemstones and all the colors of the rainbow—no, all the colors of the world. My sense of it is that the various hues of the stones are meant to convey the beauty as well as the diversity of the races and nations that make up the incredible spectacle we know as the people of God.

Under the old covenant between God and humanity described in the Bible, the temple was critical because it was where God was. Under the new covenant that Jesus brought in, the people are the temple of God because it is within his people that he dwells. The old Jerusalem, which is still with us, is important to many because its bricks and stones and streets have seen David and Jesus. The new Jerusalem is not about bricks and stones and streets. It is made up of the people who have believed in and worshiped and loved the Lamb of God. In the midst of them is God. As he walked among his people in Eden, so he will walk among them in Second Eden.

I saw the Holy City, the new Jerusalem, coming down out of heaven from God, prepared as a bride beautifully dressed for her husband. And I heard a loud voice from

the throne, saying, "Look! God's dwelling place is now among the people, and he will dwell with them. They will be his people, and God himself will be with them and be their God. He will wipe every tear from their eyes. There will be no more death or mourning or crying or pain, for the old order of things has passed away.
Revelation 21:2–4 TNIV

The unity between God and his people, ruptured at First Eden, is restored at Second Eden. The pain that afflicted the earth because of the break between humanity and divinity ceases to exist. Death that came with banishment from First Eden is itself banished from Second Eden. First Eden and its influence, for good or ill, are done. Now the only Eden is Second Eden, and the only reality is its reality: human anguish is no more. "How great a Fall that merited so great a Redemption," wrote Augustine. We might add, "How great a loss that merited so great a restoration." Second Eden is infinitely more splendid and complete than its predecessor.

FIVE

The garden we are given a glimpse of proves how much greater Second Eden is than the original. First Eden had one tree of life; Second Eden has two. There was a river in First Eden that watered the garden and also split into four rivers that watered the earth. But the river in Second Eden is purer; it is as clear as crystal. It is the river of the water of life, a symbol of Christ and eternity, and it flows directly from the throne of God and the Lamb. Its source and its vitality are divine. It flows through the heart of God's people, down the middle of the city's street, and brings water to all. It nourishes the two trees of life, and in doing so, it nourishes the entire earth in the most potent of ways: the leaves of the trees heal all the nations, and every month there is a fresh crop of divine and edible fruit.

> Then the angel showed me the river of the water of life, as clear as crystal, flowing from the throne of God and of the Lamb down the middle of the great street of the city. On each side of the river stood the tree of life, bearing twelve crops of fruit, yielding its fruit every month. And the leaves of the trees are for the healing of the nations.
>
> Revelation 22:1–2

The possibility of evil and sin existed in First Eden. Not so in Second Eden: "No longer will there be any curse" (22:3). The glory of God is the sun and moon, and the Lamb is the light. The nations no longer have the possibility of going about their business in the shadows; they will walk completely in the light of God (21:24). All their goodness will fill the garden. There is no such thing as the dark night of the soul anymore, for spiritual night is not an aspect of the final garden (21:25; 22:5). A sea of evil will swamp no one. The polluted skies and seas and land of the world we know, physically and spiritually, will vanish, and fresh air and unspoiled land and waters will take their place (21:1).

It will be a brand-new start for everything and everyone — a second Genesis, a whole new beginning for planet Earth. "He who was seated on the throne said, 'I am making everything new!'" (21:5). And he echoes the words of the Lamb on the cross: "It is done" (21:6). It is accomplished. God is with his people forever. Nothing will come between them. It is the Age of Immanuel, an age with no time frame and no limitations. Now it is always Christmas morning.

SIX

Mister Buon Giorno created his world in his backyard. When you think about it, many of us do the same — whether it is a city or town, village or hamlet, or just a cluster of huts or trailers. Second Eden, the garden at the beginning of the new world, is like that — a garden in a city, a garden with limits, a garden with gates and a perimeter. But it does not stay put. It spills over the fence and out through the gate and covers the whole earth. It is a global garden. It is a new heaven and a new earth. Its borders are the stars.

The way I see it, the Bible is one long, rambling story from beginning to end, complete with princes and princesses, wicked kings and queens (as well as good ones), dragons, spells, ghosts, angels, wise men with staffs, God in a human body, animals that talk, birds that feed heroes in hiding, battles to the death, sparkling acts of kindness, miracles, magic blood, monstrous evil from the pit of hell, and all of it the honest-to-God truth.

The end of the story is a wonderful green place brimming with flowers and goodness and peace where the people of the earth, in all their gemlike colors of skin, walk about and greet one another in the shimmering light of an eternal spring. The best thing is that no one closes the book and sends you to bed or tells you to forget the stories — that it's time to grow up. Or shakes you awake and says it was just a dream. This story is forever, and this story is the one true story that holds all others in its hands. This is the one to die for.

I'm astonished that so many feel uncomfortable when we talk about God telling stories, or when we speak of Jesus' parables as fictions he thought up. For truth is truth, whether it is carried by a storyteller or by someone with news to tell. Fiction and story can bring us to God as quickly as the stories of real life.

Story carries the Bible on its back. Often enough, the stories give us a better sense of God's truth than all the words we use when we try to unpack them. A person can go on forever, explaining what it means when we say that the end of the world is a garden of God. And there is nothing wrong with that. There is a place for that. We like to talk about it. But just to describe the power and beauty and fertility of the garden itself conjures up pictures in people's minds that are as strong and bright as the truth the garden symbolizes.

Which tells us more? To speak the words "God is love" or to tell the story of the prodigal son and loving father (Luke 15:11 – 32)? To say, "If you persist in prayer, eventually God will answer," or to say, "In a certain town there was a judge who neither feared God nor cared what people thought. And there was a widow in that town who kept coming to him with the plea, 'Grant me justice against my adversary'" (Luke 18:2 – 3 TNIV)? Is it better to say, "God will nurture you both now and in the world to come," or to say, "You are a garden, and God is the gardener who prizes you"? Stories are the silver dollars that jingle in the denim pocket of God — the God who came to earth and put on our clothes and walked our streets and talked our talk.

At En Gedi, in the Song of Songs, we first understood that the bride was the garden, that we are the garden. This was reinforced by Jesus in the gospels, who said he is the vine, and we are the branches (John 15:5); in other words, that he is a garden and because of that we are a garden too. And then, in Revelation, in Second Eden, right through the heart of the bride, right through us, runs the water of life that nourishes immortality (the tree of life) and the new life of the nations (the leaves of the tree).

It is not only in Revelation that we get this image of the people of God as a garden that has enough life-giving water to make it expansive and lush and fertile. Moses, Isaiah, and Jeremiah offer the same image and the same truth:

How beautiful are your tents, O Jacob,
your dwelling places, O Israel!

Like valleys they spread out,
like gardens beside a river,
like aloes planted by the LORD,
like cedars beside the waters.

Numbers 24:5–6

You will be like a well-watered garden,
like a spring whose waters never fail.

Isaiah 58:11

They will come and shout for joy on the heights of Zion;
they will rejoice in the bounty of the LORD —
the grain, the new wine and the oil,
the young of the flocks and herds.

They will be like a well-watered garden,
  and they will sorrow no more.

Jeremiah 31:12

The people of God are like valleys, gardens beside a river, cedars beside the waters, well-watered gardens, a spring whose waters never fail. The pictures that form in the mind convey a cluster of great truths to the heart. The people of God are beautiful. They are strong. They are full of grace. They are full of growth. They are full of life. They are unending. These images make hope easier, and faith and worship and prayer as well. They give joy more freedom. And love. A person brims with peace as he or she contemplates these images — pictures that have the power to restore the soul.

SEVEN

But what good to us now is a Second Eden that is not yet, a place in which holy waters flow between trees that grant eternal life? The same good as a heaven that is not yet. We look at it from a distance. It helps us focus. It gives perspective. Offers a goal. Lifts our heads and refreshes our eyes. It reminds us that the spiritual life is not just about right now or next month and that it is not limited by our damaged legs, our deafness or blindness, our aging bodies, our brittling bones. Death does not have the final say, and all our prayers and visions and tears in the night do not end with a grave cut out of the ground or with the fires of cremation. Looking at the colors of Second Eden, at the healing of nations that once warred against each other, at faces free of grief and despair, at Godlight as sunlight and moonlight and lamplight, we get a strong sense of moving toward something that matters, a reality that is going to make a difference—that we are part of something that is world changing, our existence has a purpose out of all proportion to our size or salary or self-esteem. Our life and death are in the presence of what awes and transforms and ignites the night. We have both a destiny and a destination, and it is all one piece—body and soul, Father, Son, Holy Spirit, new heaven, new earth, new Eden.

The tree of life turns out to be a cross. But the cross itself becomes the tree of life, and Christ's wounds its leaves: "He himself bore our sins in his body on the tree, so that we might die to sins and live for righteousness; by his wounds you have been healed" (1 Peter 2:24). The gardens connect. There is a common path between them all. The cuttings from one thrive in the soil of another. We are included in the final garden because of the Lamb, but the Lamb is in the final garden only because he was in the other gardens first. The gardens are not just symbols or metaphors of the truth; they are truth itself. What happens to us when we enter into them and pray makes all the difference in the world.

The decisions Jesus made in Gethsemane affected all of us. Gethsemane is more than a symbol. What happened to Jesus in the Garden Tomb affected our entire universe. The Garden Tomb is more than a story. What will happen to humanity and all heaven and earth in Second Eden impacts everyone and everything. Second Eden is more than an image. The biblical gardens are physical realities and spiritual realities, but they are also decision realities, vision realities, and encounter realities. When you go to them, they will work on you. If you stay in any one of them long enough, you will dream dreams and see visions. You will pray prayers you've never prayed, make choices you've never considered. You will encounter good, and you will encounter evil, not only in the garden space around you but in the garden space within you.

You may come face-to-face with summer lightning and realize it is an angel. You may come face-to-face with Jesus but at first think you are seeing a gardener. The gardens are volatile places. You may find rest in one or two of them, but nothing in any of the gardens is at rest. Flowers are opening and closing. Seeds sprouting. Fruit taking shape. Those who come to the gardens cannot expect to remain untouched. If everything around you is growing, you will eventually come to grow yourself. What this will look like God only knows. But if it is God you are looking for, it is God you will find. For these are his gardens. He waters and cultivates and prunes them. It is your soil he has turned. Your seed he has planted.

The gardener will never neglect or fail to cherish what is his own.

THE CHRIST PATH

Would you be able to make a garden path?"
It's one thing to talk about the garden path; it's another thing to create one. But my wife had already started making a pathway along one side of the house. It was my turn to try to do something with the garden itself.

This was the same garden that had been killed by a flood and then resurrected. In one section, strawberries were trying to make a comeback. In another, it was a patch of raspberries. In yet another, herbs such as tarragon and thyme and sage. In my grandfather's day, you simply slapped down a few boards to walk on between the rows. But this garden deserved something better.

I went to a gardening center and purchased round red stones about a foot across and placed a dozen of them in the garden. But I needed more. So I bought some steel butterfly squares and a steel dragonfly round. This made it possible to move fairly easily around the plants in the garden, but there were still some trouble spots. So I began to use stones from the creek, as flat and smooth as I could find. I dug shallow holes for each stone and pressed them firmly into the soil. After a few hours it was possible for me to walk between the raspberry canes without getting scratched and to examine the echinacea and daisies and sunflowers without crushing other plants as I did so.

We are at the far eastern edge of a town nestled only a few

miles from the Rocky Mountains in southwestern Alberta. Our house is encircled by a yard that provides us with solitude, even though we are right next to a small highway. A creek with headwaters in the mountains runs through our property. The backyard that rims the creek is thick with trees—cottonwood, poplar, and elm, as well as white pine and Colorado blue spruce. Birds fill the treetops—great horned owls, kingfishers, northern flickers, blue jays, mountain chickadees, and nuthatches, to name a few. Deer walk through autumn leaves so thick on the ground at times I use a large snow shovel to clear the leaves up. Rainbow and native cutthroat trout swim in the current; a chocolate-brown mink scurries up and down the creek bank. A friend told me it was like visiting a nature reserve whenever he dropped by.

"What I know of the divine sciences and Holy Scriptures," said Bernard of Clairvaux, "I learned in woods and fields. I have no other masters than the beeches and the oaks." I look at the tall spruces and the gnarly-fisted cottonwoods, some of which were undoubtedly here 150 years ago, when buffalo roamed through what is now our yard, and I find myself wondering about the personality behind the making of them. What is a person like who thinks up stars and comets and redwoods and mule deer and whitewater and wild rosebushes?

Then I think of Jesus and his stories that told of earth and trees and plants and seeds. The treasure hidden in the field, for instance. The workers in the vineyard who came late in the day and got the same pay as those who worked through the heat of the day. The rich fool with all his fields and crops and barns.

The sower and the seeds scattered in various places and having various fates. The wheat growing together with the weeds or tares until the harvest. The son who says he'll work in the fields but doesn't and the son who says he won't work in the fields but thinks better of it and does. The mustard seed that grows into the largest plant in the garden. The fig tree that blossoms and the fig tree that does not. The owner of a vineyard whose own son is killed trying to collect some of the produce that is owed to the family.

And there is the miracle of the garden: "This is what the kingdom of God is like. A man scatters seed on the ground. Night and day, whether he sleeps or gets up, the seed sprouts and grows, though he does not know how" (Mark 4:26–27). Of course, one of the reasons Jesus tells so many stories about seeds and fields and plants and vineyards is that he was talking to people who knew all about such things. Many of them made their living at it. But I think another reason is that God envisioned soil and seeds to be symbols of the spiritual world long before our planet existed. It is only natural that Jesus would use them to discuss good and evil and God and the human soul. It's one of the things they were designed for. And it is in the family and in the blood. Jesus is a gardener. Just like his Father.

The garden that rose from the dead in my backyard almost died a second death in the course of the writing of this book. Neglected while my wife and I were busy at other things, it survived the summer only by the grace of God. With a July and August of rainstorms and heat, the garden, without any assistance on our part, remained lush. If there hadn't been enough rain, the heat most certainly would have scorched the garden, and neither Linda nor I would have noticed until it was too late.

I did not have much chance to look at the garden closely until the autumn. I pulled a few weeds (surprisingly there weren't that many), hoed the soil to loosen it, and when the harvest moon shone went out and sat in the white light. As I thought and prayed, I noticed the echinacea at my shoulder, taller than my head, its peculiar cone-shaped flower nudging me whenever a warm breeze stirred the garden. Off to my left, high stalks of tarragon swayed. At the time I was reading about the monastic herb garden and said out loud, in a flash of realization, "I have never harvested these herbs." The next day, my son complained of a sore throat and I made him a tea of lavender, sage, marjoram, and tarragon—I had read that tarragon, in particular, was rich in vitamin C. An hour after having two cups, he excitedly told me his sore throat had gone from a seven to a one on the pain scale. My daughter's experience was much the same. Tired, her throat raw, starting to blow her nose, she drank cup after cup of echinacea and thyme. A day later she felt 99 percent.

As the hunter's moon that year began to wax in shape and strength, I decided time was running out on harvesting the herbs and bringing them indoors to dry for winter use. One sunny Saturday, I cut and bundled them and hung them up in the garage. The lavender soon filled the space with sweetness so sweet I decided to move them inside to hang, like unusual dry flower arrangements, in our living room. Echinacea and marjoram were on the brick wall by the wood stove, tarragon swept across a wall on the other side of the room, thyme rested in a woven basket, lavender lay in a bowl of myrtlewood and rose up out of a second bowl of handmade pottery. (I did leave some lavender in the garage because our Alaskan Malamutes sleep there and I'm quite sure they liked the smell.)

A lunar eclipse occurred that week, and I stood in the yard thinking about Jesus and his prayers in Gethsemane and his full moon of Passover. Our moon, perfectly round that night, turned pink and then a smoky red. Stars that were washed out by moonlight only minutes before gleamed like gemstones. Strange colors and shadows and lights moved about in my garden. It is easy to see Gethsemane on such a night. Easy to think about all the biblical gardens and everything that is in them. God and eternity become much more obvious on a night when the moon is dark—and the dark is the color of blood.

I glanced at a small rosebush that emerged near one of the garden pathways. The plant had never done very well. It scarcely produced blossoms from one year to the next, but I kept it because a good friend had given it to my wife and me as a gift. Just a scraggly little rosebush—yet under the blood moon it seemed to take on a size and grandeur that were never apparent in the light of day. And I thought of a story.

Suppose such a scraggly rosebush grew in the courtyard of the majestic castle of a great king and queen. And suppose all the other roses and flowers that grew around it were lush and full of color. And suppose people always talked about getting rid of the ugly rosebush, but the old gardener would not let them because the rosebush·had been a gift from a good friend of the king.

Then suppose great darkness swept over the land. It was

always night, with no moon and no stars and never a sunrise. And cold—great cold that froze pails of water and killed newborn calves before the farmers could rescue them. And violence—horrible violence that seized the land by the throat and choked the life and the peace and the joy from it.

Then suppose a tale was unearthed from the old books that prophesied just such a catastrophe in the kingdom. And that the only way to end the curse of darkness was to make the scraggly rosebush, said to be found in the king's own garden, blossom. And the only way to do that was to water it with blood.

But not just any blood. A magic blood. From a person who probably had no idea they carried within his or her veins a blood that had powers far beyond the powers of armies and kings.

It was not hard to get people to throng to the castle from all over the kingdom to have a finger pricked and three drops of blood squeezed onto the scraggly rosebush. After all, what were three drops of blood? And the king had promised that whoever had the magic blood that would cause the rose to flourish, thus turning darkness into light, would sit at his right hand in the throne room. If a man, he would marry his lovely daughter; if a woman, she would marry his handsome son. And there would also be a chest full of rubies and sapphires and diamonds for the one whose blood unraveled the curse.

So for weeks they came; for months they came. Some days, the line of men and women and children who stood to have their fingers cut and their blood carefully dripped onto the rosebush stretched for miles. Yet in spite of all the people who came and went, nothing changed. The bush remained stunted and without blossoms; the darkness remained impenetrable and without stars.

Now it was the custom to close the castle gates once the hourglasses had measured out a passage of time that was the equivalent of one day. This allowed everyone to get some rest and relief from the constant babble of excited voices and the clamor of braying donkeys and squealing cartwheels. And it so happened that one night, after everyone had fallen asleep, including those lined up in front of the rosebush who simply slept where they were, a young boy came running by on an important errand.

He was the son of the king's farrier — not handsome, not tall, but a pleasant enough lad, quiet, with only a few friends, and a great help to his father. He was delivering to one of the princes some horseshoes that his father had just completed. As the boy returned from the prince's chamber, a silver coin in his pocket, he walked quietly past all those huddled and asleep beside the rosebush. He stopped to look at the scraggly bush. It seemed dead to him. How could such a plant restore light to the kingdom, blood or no blood? He reached out his hand to touch its gray branches.

Ow! He pulled his hand back, but not before the thorns had drawn blood. He grimaced and put his finger to his mouth. A guard began to approach from the direction of the gate, and the boy walked swiftly away into the shadows, sucking on his cut.

Within minutes, the guard was hammering on the door to the king's bedchamber.

"My lord, come quickly!" he shouted.

"Who disturbs the king?" came an angry voice from within.

"I am with the night watch. My lord, come quickly!"

"What is it?"

"The rose has blossomed!"

Hastily throwing on a few garments, the king and queen flew from their room and down the steps to the courtyard. Already, people were awake and stumbling away from the scraggly rosebush in fear and amazement. For it was scraggly no longer—it was seven feet high and thick with leaves and crimson roses as big around as a man's fist. From it shone an unearthly light that burned through the darkness like fire. The entire courtyard was filled with a brightness that caused people to shout and shriek and fling their arms up over their eyes. Within minutes, the sky over their heads was blue, and in the east a yellow sun rose in magnificence over the fields and villages and rivers of the kingdom.

People began to cheer and clap and dance, but all the time the king and queen were looking at the people in the courtyard and crying, "Who did it? Who? Whose blood?" But there was so much noise and excitement no one heard them.

And then, as sunlight and warmth flooded the land and people wept for joy to see the green grass and blue streams and white clouds, one man came forward and bowed and said, "Your majesty, it was my finger. See the cut here."

But the king looked at the man and frowned. "No, it was not you," he said.

Then a woman came forward and curtsied to the queen. "Your majesty," she smiled, "I must tell you that it was I."

The queen shook her head. "No," she said quickly, "it was not you."

More and more people pressed in on the king and queen and cried, "It was I, it was I," but the king and queen knew better and answered them again and again, "No, it was not," and the guards thrust the crowd back.

Suddenly over the yelling and shouting and tumult came a sharp wail of grief that chilled everyone to the bone and silenced every voice.

"Where is that coming from?" demanded the king.

"From the farrier's hut," answered a woman.

The king and queen and all the people rushed to the hut and found the farrier and his wife leaning over their son in tears. The farrier looked up, his face contorted with pain.

"I went to wake him up, my lord," he groaned, "to show him the sun, but he would not stir, and now he is as stiff and cold as ice."

The king kneeled by the boy and opened his left hand—nothing. Then he opened the right, and on the forefinger he saw the tiny cut from the thorn. The king sat back, tears running down his face.

"So this boy has saved us," he whispered, his voice barely audible he was so choked with emotion. "I had begun to doubt the prophecies were true. I even doubted the words that said the one who gave his blood would give his life, so I told no one but my queen."

The queen held the mother in her arms as she sobbed. The king stood. Then he turned to his servants.

"Go," he said, "fetch my finest robe and wrap this boy in it. Call my bravest men to put on full armor and bear the boy like a prince to the garden in which all the kings of the kingdom lie. There bury him among the roses and the lilacs and the white lilies and let him sleep the sleep of the great. For of all who take their rest in the royal garden there is none greater than this boy, the farrier's son."

Then suppose that while the kingdom simultaneously rejoiced at the return of the light and mourned the loss of the young boy, the wise man who kept the old books deep in the bowels of the castle watched and wondered, for he knew there were other words too, words no one had noticed in a book no one remembered. And the wise man considered that if the words about the blood and the death had come true, so might the words about the return to life.

We know this story, do we not? Jesus not only lived this story; he told his own version of it when he gave us the parable of the man who rents out his vineyard to tenants and then goes on a long journey. Every person the man sends to collect his share of the harvest they beat and turn away. When he sends his own son, they throw him out of the vineyard and kill him (Luke 20:9–19).

C. S. Lewis told his own version of this tale also. Many of us know it well. The sons and daughters of Adam, Aslan the lion, the White Witch, the Stone Table—we know Lewis's version of Christ's Passion as the story called "The Lion, The Witch, and The Wardrobe."

The story of the rosebush I've just related is another retelling of Christ's death and resurrection. Why do we tell so many stories about a story that really happened? Why not just tell the story itself? Because sometimes in the telling and retelling of a familiar event we begin to lose something. Sometimes it takes a retelling in a slightly different way to help us see the heart of the real story once again. Sometimes it takes a retelling to allow us to hear the real story as though we are hearing it for the first time.

We tell stories so that truths that have been forgotten are found, so that what is difficult to understand is made plain, and sometimes so that what is taken for granted as being so straightforward and obvious is rendered not so obvious and not so straightforward. Jesus' own stories are like that. So are the stories of the gardens we have just walked through.

Each garden talks to us in different ways — one tells a story of death, another of love, yet another of life out of death. Each story is true, each perspective is valuable, each story differs from the other, yet each story is the same — the gardens are all about God and the gardens are all about us and the gardens are all about God bringing us close to himself through his Son. The gardens are timeless. So are the stories they tell. And sometimes they are the best places to go to hear the words and stories we need to hear when the words and stories from other places aren't touching our hearts and souls the way we need to be touched.

The garden path takes us to different parts of the garden. Columbine here, raspberries there — each is a different experience. So the path of our lives will wind and twist its way to many different gardens: Gethsemane one week, En Gedi the next month, Eden the next year. We need the different gardens, the different stories, the different ways God can reach us, because we have so many different experiences in a week, in a year, in a lifetime. Yet the believer in God and Christ must remember that ultimately all the gardens are one because they are God's gardens, and he is the one who tends them. And the believer must also remember that although there are many paths through these gardens of death and life, ultimately there is only one path through all the gardens of God.

That path is Christ—the Way, the Truth, the Life.

ACKNOWLEDGMENTS

No man, no woman writes alone. Not ever. Thanks, Eugene, for your friendship and prayers and the well-wrought words of your foreword to this book. Thanks to my agent, Les Stobbe, who has been such an encouragement and support over the past few years. Thanks also to the great editorial team I've worked with at HarperCollins and Zondervan, especially Andy Meisenheimer and Dirk Buursma. It means a lot to know you guys believe in my writing.

Thanks also to Tom Dean in marketing, always ready with a warm word and an answer for my questions. For my wife, Linda, and my children, Micah and Micaela, your love and faith and many kindnesses help me to keep going — for though a writer has many friends, it is still a lonely business and would be much less enjoyable without the heart and soul of the fantastic family you surround me with. And to John Launstein, a friend who helped me revise *Rooted* from an earlier manuscript — thanks for all your hard work. It made a difference.

In the end, thank God, for it's been a long journey, and it's very good to be here.

Streams

Reflections on the Waters in Scripture

Murray Andrew Pura

Mingling personal anecdotes with scriptural wisdom, author and pastor Murray Andrew Pura explores the many ways water is portrayed in the Bible. Readers will meditate on:

- The Red Sea's challenging waters: How do we conquer obstacles?

- The rivers of Babylon and their waters of darkness: How do we handle tragedy and suffering?

- Streams in the desert and the waters of rejuvenation: What do we do when our spiritual lives are dry?

- And much, much more

This refreshing new book will help readers discover the deeper meanings of water in Scripture and better understand the life-giving power of a Christian life.

Hardcover, Printed: 978-0-310-31838-5

Pick up a copy at your favorite bookstore or online!

ZONDERVAN®
.com

Share Your Thoughts

With the Author: Your comments will be forwarded to the author when you send them to *zauthor@zondervan.com*.

With Zondervan: Submit your review of this book by writing to *zreview@zondervan.com*.

Free Online Resources at
www.zondervan.com

Zondervan AuthorTracker: Be notified whenever your favorite authors publish new books, go on tour, or post an update about what's happening in their lives at www.zondervan.com/authortracker.

Daily Bible Verses and Devotions: Enrich your life with daily Bible verses or devotions that help you start every morning focused on God. Visit www.zondervan.com/newsletters.

Free Email Publications: Sign up for newsletters on Christian living, academic resources, church ministry, fiction, children's resources, and more. Visit www.zondervan.com/newsletters.

Zondervan Bible Search: Find and compare Bible passages in a variety of translations at www.zondervanbiblesearch.com.

Other Benefits: Register yourself to receive online benefits like coupons and special offers, or to participate in research.